# From Disposable Culture
# to Disposable People

# From Disposable Culture to Disposable People

The Unintended Consequences of Plastics

SASHA ADKINS

*Foreword by Noel Moules*

RESOURCE *Publications* · Eugene, Oregon

FROM DISPOSABLE CULTURE TO DISPOSABLE PEOPLE
The Unintended Consequences of Plastics

Resource Publications
An Imprint of Wipf and Stock Publishers
199 W. 8th Ave., Suite 3
Eugene, OR 97401

www.wipfandstock.com

PAPERBACK ISBN: 978-1-5326-4990-5
HARDCOVER ISBN: 978-1-5326-4991-2
EBOOK ISBN: 978-1-5326-4992-9

Manufactured in the U.S.A.                    DECEMBER 18, 2018

*for Joseph*

# Contents

# List of Tables and Illustrations

# Foreword

NOEL MOULES

PLASTIC PROMISED SO MUCH. Today, how can it be so out of control? It gives with one hand, while wrecking havoc scientifically, socially and spiritually with the other. It is this reality Sasha Adkins' powerful book grapples with: both the physical problem of plastic, plus those much bigger issues that are inextricably entangled with it.

Nothing on our planet escapes the presence of plastic. It is in the air, water and soil. Every town and city on Earth—everything—whether it is our vast global wildernesses, or the depths of the human heart, each is contaminated in some life-challenging way by its presence. Our ocean wildernesses, already awash with tens of trillions of pieces of plastic in every form, receive a further eight million metric tons every year—the equivalent of one full garbage truck of plastic *each minute*. Recently, crustaceans collected from the bottom of the Mariana Trench—seven miles deep—had *all* eaten plastic. It is estimated that by 2050 there will be more plastic in the oceans than fish. By the same date the global production of plastics is projected to have increased by 500%.[1] These truths are simply as overwhelming as they are horrific.

1. Some statistics from Sasha Adkins' text, others from BBC Documentary 'Drowning In Plastic'- https://www.bbc.co.uk/iplayer/episode/bobmbn47/ drowning-in-plastic—UK broadcast Monday 1st October 2018. Executive Producer: Dominique Walker, Presenter: Liz Bonnin.

However—as I hinted above—Sasha Adkins' book is a great deal more than a voice crying out about what a plexiform plague plastic has become. In their own words, "When I began my exploration into plastics, they were mere molecules . . . Now they have become more potent to me as symbols of a culture that views both the material world and the living world—even people—instrumentally, as though they are disposable resources . . . This is not a story about simply following intellectual curiosity. It is also about my struggle to understand what to do with all of this information, and with the rage and pain that I feel seeing some of the consequences of disposable culture."

*This is a powerfully prophetic book.*

I use this term in its true biblical sense: identifying someone who stands up apart from the crowd, while at the same time capturing and holding the attention of the crowd. Proclaiming truth to whole populations, while at the same time directing it towards those *with* power and *in* power. Setting out the issues in all their stark disturbing detail, yet in doing so calling out to that deep moral awareness which is woven into the very fabric of what it actually means to be human. Naming the perilous consequences of indifference, while at the same time offering hope – but only if there is radical and sustained change. Sasha Adkins does not fail at any point.

As a polymer scientist Sasha Adkins carefully introduces us to this shape-shifting world of plastics with their seemingly infinite uses and applications. I urge you to follow them attentively as they take us by the hand and lead us through this bewildering maze of molecular mutations signposted by often unpronounceable and equally incomprehensible names. This is an important path to tread, as they slowly reveal the toxic impact of plastics in a multitude of different and shocking ways. Whether it is their invisible contamination of our environments, or their deliberate use to falsify products, such as rice extended with shreds of polyethylene. Or the irresponsible and indifferent attitude of both industries and governments towards the production of plastics, as in the case of the Aamjiwnaang (Chippewa) First Nation who find themselves at the heart of 'Chemical Valley' in Sarnia, Ontario—where 40% of Canada's chemical industry is based, including sixty plastics and chemical manufacturers—which have sprung up around them like a ring of toxic toadstools embedding themselves on these traditional aboriginal lands. Without the slightest concern for the health and social issues they inflict across the generations of the Indigenous population.

Sasha Adkins' rage is palpable, so also is their deep compassion. They recognize that their study of plastics has become a powerfully useful tool for making the case that toxins are both civil rights and human rights issues. For them, black lives matter, Indigenous lives matter, and undocumented lives matter—so too do those of white "trailer-trash." How can we have come to think, speak and treat other human beings in this way? Everything and everyone has become disposable. "It is simply our culture," we shrug. No wonder we have a global environmental crisis.

*This is a deeply spiritual book.*

"In this lonely and broken world, where do I look for God? I chose to start in the trash pile." For me, this simple, disturbing yet profound statement distils the essence of the whole book.

Sasha Adkins reminds us that nature has no waste. Everything flows in endless cycles of energy expressed in infinite forms; nothing ever diminished or lost, an eternal cascade of abundance pouring over and through everything that is. 'Trash,' 'rubbish,' and 'garbage' are each human creations and concepts with disturbing origins and consequences; just one of the many tragic demonstrations of our failure to live in harmony with and within the cosmos, plus irrefutable proof that the ecological crisis is first and foremost a spiritual crisis.

God as garbage, Jesus as junk, Spirit as scrap—a trinity of trash—with creation viewed as crap (with so many individuals also feeling exactly the same way about themselves); everyone and everything now free to be exploited at will, is the choice so much of Western culture continues to believe it is free to make. Yes, I recognise these are strong statements. I give no apology. They are truly expressive of how many people—consciously or unconsciously—feel and think today, as this book makes clear. In contrast the spiritual, with its focus on *meaning* and *relationship*, challenges all this and offers a different path. Yet so frequently it is ignored, leaving fragmenting plastic, people and the planet herself in its wake.

Sasha Adkins reminds us that—in the Torah story—it is only when Balaam recognizes his donkey as an *individual* to be respected, rather than something *instrumental* that can simply be replaced, does he see the angel. Our disposable culture has blinded us to both the divine and the sacred value of *all* things. Culturally and spiritually we are each in urgent need of a 'Balaam moment'.

With this in mind—for me personally[2]—the single most transformational encounter in this book, and in Sasha Adkins' teaching as a whole, is when they tell of the occasion they asked a group of their students to each find a piece of trash tossed in the breeze, and then make it the center of their focus in prayer and meditation for a whole week. Slowly they discovered the beauty in garbage. Inexplicably, raw emotions were stirred through this process, inspiring them to seek reconciliation with people from whom they had become estranged. Trash is a sacrament. Trash is as much an expression of the sacred and the holy as any forest flower or wilderness stream. Here we have a vital dimension of Jesus' declaration, "This is my body." Reflecting on this I recalled how early Christians believed that the following words were spoken about him:

"*He had no beauty or status to attract us, nothing in his appearance was appealing. He was despised and rejected, a person of suffering, familiar with pain. Like something from which people hide their faces, he was despised, and viewed with disgust*".[3]

---

2. What I have written is supplemented with information from Sasha Adkins '*Plastics is a Spiritual Crisis*' in Myers C [Ed] (2016) '*Watershed Discipleship: reinhabiting bioregional faith and practice*' Eugene, Oregon: Cascade Books; 164, and my personal conversation with the author.

3. Nevi'im/Isaiah 53:2-3 (my own personal paraphrase).

If God is present within the trash, then surely our desire can only be to treat with respect everything we no longer need. If what we consider as garbage is actually one expression of the body of Christ, then so many of our attitudes and responses must change. This is a call to return to first principles, to recognize everything as sacred, and then to question what and how we create from physical matter, all of which we know to be holy. This simple step will also transform our relationship with every other person including the whole 'more than human world.'[4]

*This is a significantly personal and practical book.*

Flowing through all the scientific information, detail and analysis that forms an important foundation to this book, plus all the biblical and theological reflections that are at the heart of its message, there is a very powerful personal story filled with deep passion and compassion, which on occasions expresses itself—movingly—in raw rage.

Seven of Sasha Adkins' most formative childhood and early-teen years were spent at sea on a sailboat sharing in their parents' fervor for marine adventuring. I love their comment, "My home is the Atlantic Ocean. I am from tide pools and coral reefs." They set so much into context. Their direct and sustained relationship with the vast elemental powers of nature makes them who they are—not unlike my own experience of growing up in the forests and foothills of the Himalaya.

Key moments will always remain with me. The impact of the necropsy of a dead albatross entangled in fishing gear with a digestive system filled with plastic garbage. The tiny baby of a homeless street-couple deliberately and violently ripped from Sasha's cradling arms in a police raid and left a crushed and lifeless corpse on a Kenyan sidewalk. Their personal fury in trying to reconcile their time spent on the academic study of polymers while the life of their Black transgender friend was in danger every time they walked the streets—triggered by their friend's apology for eating

---

4. The phrase 'more-than-human world' was coined by David Abram to expand our thinking, see Abram D (1996) and its title, *The Spell of the Sensuous: perception and language in a more-than-human world.*

their meal with a plastic fork. Each of these moments illustrates a step (and there are many other examples I could have quoted) on Sasha Adkins' journey as they wrestle with how to respond in our disposable culture with its inhuman 'disposable' attitude to people and the far wider world beyond humans.

There is such disarming honesty in this book. Sasha Adkins' desire—like our own—to live 'plastic free' in today's world and the seeming impossibility of the task; their struggle with guilt, the need for creativity and unyielding persistence, plus their learning from the ideas and example of others. Amid all its detail this book is *so* practical and truthful.

*Finally.* At one point those oft quoted words of Baba Dioum— the Senegalese forester, conservationist and political activist—are fleetingly alluded to, "In the end, we will conserve only what we love; we will love only what we understand and we will understand only what we are taught."[5] Sasha Adkins skillfully—with both wisdom and zeal—helps point us towards how we might actually achieve each of these three essential values, and I am grateful. This is a powerful book. It has an urgent, unique and carefully crafted message, which simply *must* be heard. So please read it, recommend it, and then together let's act on it!

*Noel Moules is the author of the book, "Fingerprints of Fire, Footprints of Peace: a spiritual manifesto from a Jesus perspective"; he is also the founder-director of Anvil Trust, which—with its twin projects 'Workshop' and 'Peacemeal'—has been inspiring radical Christian learning and living since 1983.*

5. Quoted in 1968 in a paper Baba Dioum presented in New Delhi, at the triennial meeting of the general Assembly of the International Union for the Conservation of Nature and Natural resources (IUCN).

# Acknowledgments

I WISH TO THANK Alesia Maltz, my dissertation advisor and friend, for over a decade of believing in me and in this project. My students in the first university-level course I taught, a senior capstone on plastics at the University of Vermont, inspired and encouraged me. Without justin adkins, this would never have been written. Without Brenna Doheny this would never have been finished.

# List of Abbreviations

ADHD,    Attention-deficit/ hyperactivity disorder

BPA,    Bisphenol A

DEHP,    di(2-ethylhexyl)phthalate, also called bis(2-ethylhexyl) phthalate

DES,    diethylstilbestrol

DOHaD,    Developmental Origins of Health and Disease

EDC,    Endocrine disrupting compound or endocrine disrupting contaminant

meHg,    methyl mercury

NHANES,    National Health and Nutrition Survey

NICU,    neonatal intensive care unit

PBAT,    polybutylene adipate terephthalate

PEF,    polyethylene furanoate

PET,    polyethylene terephthalate

PHAs,    polyhydroxyalkanoates

PLA,    polylactide

POPs,    persistent organic pollutants

PVC,    polyvinyl chloride

US EPA,    United States Environmental Protection Agency

UV,    ultraviolet

4R,    refuse, reduce, reuse, recycle

# 1

## Introduction

### RAINBOW CHASER, 1981

WHEN I TURNED SEVEN, my parents sold our house and furniture and bought a sailboat. She (as ships are traditionally called) was a thirty-seven-foot custom-built Tyana. "Custom-built", in this case, meant that instead of buying a boat that was ready to move aboard, we bought the *idea* of a boat. Every six months or so, there would be a heated conversation about when she would be ready. Assurances would be made, but invariably the promises were broken and we moved from apartment to apartment, waiting.

Finally, she was ready. My parents named her "Rainbow Chaser", and the little sailing dinghy we towed, naturally, was called, "Pot of Gold".

The typical American home is around 2,600 square feet. Below deck, we had just 340 square feet, for three (and at one point, four) people. This was to be our home for the next seven years.

Mine was the aft cabin, which consisted of a bunk, enclosed on all sides and above, presumably to keep the occupant from falling out of bed in rough seas, and a navigation table with a bookshelf. What was a bunk on one end was the seat for the navigation table on the other, and that was that. I did not have enough room to stand up straight or stretch out my arms. The trade-off was that I had a radio, a depth sounder, and charts (the nautical equivalent of maps) of the places we would visit.

My parents had the forward cabin, which had a large bunk under a hatch with a skylight. They had one tiny closet, which we all shared. I was given two hangers, and all of my clothes went on them, one outfit over another. Most of the other available storage space was devoted, by necessity, to more important provisions, such as canned food.

Many landlocked homes have shelves crowded with decorative curios, and kitchen counters with spice jars or cutting boards on them. In our case, every surface was, by necessity, bare. Anything I'd brought out to play with could not be set down for a moment without being secured. Even our chess set had magnets so that the pieces wouldn't slide off the board. When a ship is at sea, anything not properly stowed poses a potentially lethal hazard. It could fall on someone, or trip them, or break and cut them. I was trained to cultivate the habit of picking things up even when we were docked, and this habit has become so inculcated in me that to this day I feel anxious when things are out of place.

Midships was a living room, with two bench settees that faced each other and a fold-down table in between. Below the cushions were cubbies that were filled with cans of Spam. These provided ballast as well as incentive to not get lost at sea (I'm not a fan of Spam.) Above the settees were built-in bookshelves, on which we had a telephone and a tiny television, both of which only worked when we were docked. While we were sailing, of course, there was no electricity. (Nowadays, many ships have generators.) The radio was our only form of communication at sea. My favorite part here was the grab rails on the ceiling that would steady adults when we were underway. For me, they were ideal for climbing and dangling.

The kitchen had a sink, a miniature alcohol-powered stovetop with two burners (for summer use), and a sixteen-by-eighteen-inch cast-iron diesel stove, which doubled in winter as our heat source. The refrigerator and freezer were accessed by lifting out squares of the counter top. The trick, of course, was that you had to plan ahead everything you might need from the cold storage before beginning to cook, otherwise whatever you set on the counter would block you from opening the lids again.

The head, as a bathroom on a boat is known, had a shower, sink, and toilet. A handle allowed the contents of the toilet, after use, to be pumped directly overboard. I was taught to use no more than two squares of toilet paper at a time, to keep from clogging it. Water was very precious. We had two 150-gallon tanks, which we filled with hoses when we docked. We conserved the water in our tanks by showering in the marina when that option was available. I was allowed one glass of water each evening to use for brushing my teeth and for drinking. To this day, I can't bear to see people letting a faucet run.

Looking back, I know now that drinking water from a hose is a risky proposition. Hoses tend to be made of polyvinyl chloride, and (particularly if left out in the hot sun) they leach lead, phthalates, and other undesirable compounds that we will return to later in our story into the water. Even my dad admits that the water tasted bad.

Not only what goes in, but also what went out, worried us all. My mom told me after I'd grown up that when she had her period she used to have nightmares about the blood attracting sharks that could snatch her from the safety of the boat and devour her. Fortunately, these fears were unfounded. However, when I think of how many boats docked in the marinas, each discharging raw sewage, the part of me trained in public health cringes. I came across this factoid: "A single weekend boater flushing untreated sewage into our waters produces the same amount of bacterial pollution as ten thousand people whose sewage passes through a treatment plant."[1] Fortunately, these days, boats typically use "marine sanitation devices" that either treat the waste or store it for later transfer.

Speaking of generating pollution, we stayed warm in winter by burning either diesel in the kitchen stove (from the same tank of diesel that we used to power the motor), or by burning coal in the secondary "fireplace" in the living room that vented to the deck through a small metal chimney. Needless to say, our exhaust was not filtered. One icy morning we woke up to find ourselves completely covered in soot. The stove had backdrafted. After we scrubbed off the black grime in our cold-water-only shower, my mom took me out for the day. My dad stayed below to take the fireplace chimney apart. He discovered that the creosote was so

1. Self, "Marinas".

thick that it had almost entirely occluded the flue. After he cleaned up the mess, he decided we'd switch to Duraflame logs, sawed into thirds to fit our tiny fireplace.

My favorite places were above deck. We were ringed by life-lines, which gave us something to grab onto when we were underway. There were mazes of cubbies in the cockpit, some of which were large enough for me to hide in. These cubbies held ropes, which we called "lines." I practiced coiling and tying knots, many of which were taught with mnemonics like, "the rabbit comes out of the hole, around the tree, sees a fox, and goes back into the hole" (that's for a bowline).

When we were docked, my dad would hoist me up the Bosun's chair, nearly to the top of our fifty-five-foot mast, and let me swing from stanchion to stanchion, pretending I was on a trapeze. When night fell, there was a hammock tied to the boom. I loved to sleep right under the stars lashed into the hammock so I wouldn't fall out. All the way forward, there was a bowsprit. When we were at sea, I would spend hours curled up on the bag that held the jib. From this post, I could safely dangle my feet and hands out to try to touch the dolphins that teased me, jumping and racing around our bow, always just out of reach.

At this point, all my parents knew of sailing was from the warships my father had served aboard while in the Navy, and, at the other end of the size spectrum, from the sailing classes they were both taking in dinghies in the Charles River in Boston. We preserved the traditional nautical hierarchy (euphemistically known as teamwork). My father was the Captain of our ship, my mother the Admiral. I was First Mate. It was critical that crew not question the orders of their superiors while underway. Lives were at stake. I often felt my parents took this a bit too far.

While my father learned to navigate with a sextant, my mother learned to cook a Thanksgiving turkey in a toaster oven (the trick is to take a measuring tape with you to the grocery store because, as she learned the hard way, you can't saw off the protruding parts while the bird is frozen). I learned not to romanticize Nature.

Survival while sailing demands a certain level of hypervigilance. To this day, subtle changes in the light in the room where I'm sleeping will wake me. These were the days before we delegated our awareness of our surroundings to computerized instrumentation. Keeping watch meant standing in the cockpit, at the helm, making sure that we stayed on course—holding the wheel, glancing down at the compass, and compensating for any shifts in wind direction or currents. But more importantly, it meant noticing any variation in the repetitive rhythm of waves against the hull, or in the sounds of the wind in the sails.

Sometimes there were strange noises in the night. My favorite was the snort of a whale coming up for a breath (when whales open their blowholes, they expel water before taking a breath). My mom describes standing watch one night and having the unsettling feeling that she was not alone. She turned and looked right into the eye of an orca who had surfaced to check us out. She recalls thinking, "I better be quiet, this is not my place."

My most memorable sail was a voyage to Bermuda—one week with no land in sight. However, what was never out of sight was the garbage carelessly thrown overboard by the crews of the vessels in the Marion to Bermuda Cruising Yacht Race. My dad remarked that we didn't need to navigate—we could just follow the stream of Styrofoam plates floating by.

Unfortunately, it was also memorable because we hit a reef. A new friend who wanted to go diving was at the bow directing us. Being accustomed to powerboats, he thought he was being helpful when he gave instructions like, "Go right. Ok, now, stop." We'll let him off the hook for not knowing his starboard from his port, but one thing he really should have known was that a thirty-seven-foot sailboat cannot just stop. He learned that the hard way.

There was a dreadful crunching sound and the boat lurched onto her side. My cousin Allen grabbed me and held on to the lifelines to keep us both from falling overboard. My dinner went flying.

My father and Allen spent the rest of the afternoon underwater, inspecting the damage to our boat. At the time, I don't remember anyone worrying about the damage to the reef. They discovered that our keel, which was hollow, was punctured and was taking on water, but that the hull was intact. It was decided that the extensive repairs that would be necessary could be done stateside. They would sail her back and then put her in dry dock. I registered a vote of "no confidence" in this plan and declared my intention to fly to my grandparents' instead of sailing back with them. And so I did.

My grandparents and I tracked a hurricane on the evening news, knowing that it was on course to intercept my parents. These were the days before satellite phones and GPS. We were completely out of communication with them for one very long week. We had only the meteorologists' predictions to fuel our fears.

One day the phone rang and we all gathered around to hear the good news. They had made it to shore. It turned out that the extra weight of the water in the keel had stabilized the boat. If they had not hit the reef, they might not have survived the storm.

I remember my parents saying the two things nearly all sailors say when they come ashore after a blue water voyage: "Never again", and "I'm going out for a drink." Even at my age, I knew from experience that "never again" meant that in about a month they would start planning our next adventure.

Just before I started high school, we sold the boat and bought a house near Tampa Bay. Although it didn't feel like the ocean I knew—it was as warm as bathwater and nearly as shallow—there were still manatees and dolphins and stingrays to play with.

Every gift has a shadow. Mine is placelessness. When I try to count how many cities and towns I've lived in, I come up with somewhere between forty and fifty. Being a nomad in a culture where that is not the norm means that most conversations begin with what seems innocuous enough: "Where are you from?"

I've been working on an answer to that one for years. I'm told that in kindergarten my teacher anxiously informed my parents that I couldn't distinguish between reality and fantasy. Apparently, I had been asked to draw a picture of my home and my family. Standard kindergarten fare. I was expected to produce the requisite stick figures next to an apartment building or a little house, perhaps with a fence and a dog and flowers in the garden if I were artistically inclined, which I certainly am not. I confused them by instead drawing a sea turtle. I informed my teacher, using this metaphor, that we carried our house with us and we lived inside. I refused to recant when she insisted that I was making it up. My teacher was even more befuddled when my parents corroborated my story.

"We only save the places we love, we only love the places we know . . ." has become a mantra in the field of environmentalism. Teachers strive through "place-based learning" to cultivate a "sense of place". Without this, we are told, our prognosis is poor for developing an ethic of stewardship.

My home is the Atlantic Ocean. I am from tide pools and coral reefs. My watershed consists of more than eighty-two million billion gallons and touches four continents.

You may be tempted to pass judgment on my parents for recklessly exposing their child to danger, for taking risks without appreciating the consequences, and for indulging their own thirst for adventure over precaution. What I will attempt to illustrate in the chapters that follow is that these accusations are just as aptly leveled against a society that relies on disposable plastic.


## NECROPSY, 2008

I knew the bird was frozen. Even so, when I stroked the belly feathers of the juvenile black-footed albatross on the table in front of me, its magnificent wings reaching wider than I am tall, I held my breath. It seemed poised to fly. I knew that I would probably never see one again.

The albatross is endangered. There are many reasons for this, of course. One is that the birds become entangled in long-line fishing gear, as this unfortunate one had. Another is that they are eating plastic. Up to 40 percent of the chicks do not survive. Their parents are regurgitating not food but plastic garbage. The smaller pieces fill the babies' bellies so that they lose their appetite for nutritive food and starve. The pieces that are tiny enough to be digested release poisons into their bloodstream that concentrate in their fatty tissue and interfere with their metabolism and hormone function.[2]

At Algalita Marine Research Foundation, we wondered if we could tell the story of how much plastic the birds were eating, and if we could measure the chemicals leaching from the plastic that contaminated their preen gland oil, if we might be able to advocate for source-reduction policies that would protect them.

This is how I found myself one summer day watching a scalpel slice open the belly of that beautiful albatross. This is how I found myself counting out pieces of spent ink pens and bottle caps that we pulled out of it. I contemplated the irony that it was some human child's plastic playthings that might have proven deadly to the young albatross. And I kept counting.

When it was over, I found the closest beach, hoping to find healing in the sand and the waves. Instead, I found a lot of garbage. Cigarette butts, plastic cups and forks, straws, broken bits of sand pails and toys. Much like what I'd just seen come out of the stomach of that magnificent albatross.

I went into the ice cream shop on the pier and asked if I could have a trash bag so I could collect litter. They kindly obliged. I filled up one bag so quickly that I went back for a second. And a third. I was trying to find my way out of despair by thinking, "At least this piece won't be eaten by an albatross" when I heard a mocking voice behind me call out, "Hey, bag lady, you missed one!"

I turned to face a beachgoer, who was sitting on a plastic folding chair and sipping out of a disposable plastic cup through a plastic straw. Children at his feet were using plastic shovels to scoop "sand" (which is just as likely fragments of plastic debris as it is fragments of rocks and shells these days) into plastic buckets. They were all wearing plastic flip-flops, and bathing suits made out of Lycra, which, of course, is also plastic. The girls had plastic barrettes in their hair.

---

2. Auman, "Plastic Ingestion", 239–44.

I felt myself at a turning point. If I projected my rage at him, I would never know peace. Indulging in being self-righteous and judgmental—as I know from experience—is like quicksand. It's nearly impossible to extricate myself once I start slipping. I tried to mentally reframe this as an opportunity for public education. I smiled and went over to explain to him what I'd seen in the necropsy of the bird, of the fish. He listened. I don't know what was going on in his head while he was hearing all this, or if he was simply regretting calling my attention to him in the first place, but I will say that he listened patiently and respectfully. He did not offer to help. I continued pacing and sorting—sand, shell, trash, sand, shell, seaweed, trash.

## CLEANING UP THE STREETS, 1993

A family was set up on a sidewalk in Nairobi selling oranges. As we chatted, they handed me their baby to rock. Then, someone whistled. This was a signal that the police were coming. In a moment, the other vendors had all vanished. This family could not. Their grandmother moved slowly, and perhaps my presence complicated things. The police did arrive. Suddenly, there were strong arms restraining me and a hand over my mouth to muffle my screams. The family was thrown into the back of a truck, and the baby lay smashed on the sidewalk.

When I recounted this to my host mother later that evening, she told me that the police were under orders to clean up the streets. Homeless people were considered trash. She also told me that if I ever find myself lost and am robbed, I should ask the robber for directions home, never the police. "At least the robber is human," she mused.

Today, I live in a country where to assert that Black lives matter is considered controversial.

Hundreds of undocumented immigrants die of thirst, exposure to the elements, and violence crossing the desert that connects Sonora, Mexico and Arizona, United States each year, and hundreds more disappear.[3] In the United States, researchers attribute at least 133,000 deaths a year to poverty.[4] Three hundred eighty-five million of the world's children are living in extreme poverty, subsisting on less than two US dollars a day.[5] Which of us is still human?

What does this have to do with plastic? It is humans who created the idea of waste. Nature has always had a circular economy, with nutrient cycles and energy flows. Some humans broke those cycles. The idea that some lives are more valuable than others arises from the same underlying notion that worth is a function of utility and productivity. In this worldview, value is instrumental rather than intrinsic. Things and people that no longer serve are discarded or destroyed. In order to repair the cycles on which all life depends, new technology is not enough. The spiritual contradiction must be resolved. We cannot restore ecological sustainability without also restoring the intrinsic dignity of life. Just as action follows from intention, so intentions and beliefs are shaped by our actions, as many indigenous and many faith traditions teach. Cultivating a habit of the heart in which we no longer regard things as disposable may lead to actions affirming that life is not disposable.

## WHY A BOOK ON PLASTICS?

When I began my exploration into plastics, they were mere molecules. I looked at them through a scientific lens and investigated their role as endocrine disruptors, as neurotoxicants, and as carcinogens. I explored their role in transferring contaminants into and out of the marine food web. Now they have become more potent to me as symbols of a culture that views both the material world and the living world—even people—instrumentally, as though they are disposable resources.

3. "No More Deaths".
4. "How Many U.S. Deaths".
5. "Some 385 Million Children".

The following chapters parallel this learning, but this is not a story about simply following intellectual curiosity. It is also about my struggle to understand what to do with all of this information, and with the rage and pain that I feel seeing some of the consequences of disposable culture. I began to teach, both as a form of activism and as a form of healing. This is an attempt to make the connections explicit between the scientific, societal, and spiritual dimensions of plastic, used as a proxy for disposable culture.

# 2

# The Toxicological Impacts of Plastics

## AN INTRODUCTION TO PLASTICS THEMSELVES

I WAS ONCE ACCUSED (by reputable activists) of being a spy for the plastics industry. I took it as a compliment. I had devoted a year in my doctoral program to learning the language of polymer science. The challenge was that we had no such department. I read Susan Selke and John Culter's *Plastics Packaging: Properties, Processing, Applications, and Regulations* cover to cover. I read journals and trade newsletters. In a sense, I suppose, I was spying *on* the plastics industry. If we consider polymer science a foreign language, I now know just enough to order a meal and ask directions to the bathroom. Here is your crash course.

What *are* plastics? The very word *plastic* was once complimentary. According to the Oxford English Dictionary, *plastic* was synonymous with "formative, procreative, creative". Today it is often used as a pejorative, referring to that which is "artificial, unnatural; superficial, or insincere".

When referring to the material rather than the symbolic, the term *plastic* is short for *thermoplastic*, the particular type of high molecular weight polymer that is able to shape-shift. A thermoplastic can be heated and remolded any number of times. Other types of polymers include *elastomers* (which can be stretched or deformed at room temperature, but which snap back to their original shape as soon as they are released), and *thermoset* polymers, which form irreversible chemical bonds once they cool and so cannot be reshaped.

A polymer (from the Greek *polu*, meaning many, and *meros*, meaning parts) is any chain comprised of repeating units. Sometimes just one unit repeats:

A-A-A-A-A-A

At other times, a pattern repeats:

AB-AB-AB-AB-AB

Each repeating unit is, quite logically, known as a monomer, which roughly translates as "one part". In the world of synthetic polymers, the basic monomers are ethylene, propylene, styrene, vinyl chloride, and bisphenol A (BPA). We can think of these as the building blocks of most commodity plastics. (The monomers used to make the first industrial plastic, Celluloid, were nitrocellulose and camphor; due to flammability concerns, these have fallen out of favor and are rarely used today.)

The number found in the chasing arrows symbol stamped on the bottom of many plastic containers indicates its monomer.

Table 1: Resin Codes and Monomers of the Most Common Plastics

| Code | Name of the Plastic | Monomer |
|------|---------------------|---------|
| 1 | polyethylene terephthalate | bis(2-hydroxyethyl) terephthalate |
| 2 | high density polyethylene | ethylene |
| 3 | vinyl (polyvinyl chloride) | vinyl chloride |
| 4 | low density polyethylene | ethylene |
| 5 | polypropylene | propylene |
| 6 | polystyrene | styrene |
| 7 | other (usually polycarbonate | bisphenol A |

Here is ethylene: $C_2H_4$. Ethylene occurs naturally in fruits. As they ripen, they release ethylene into the air, producing a sweet and musky fragrance. Ethylene (and propylene) that are used by industry, though, are produced synthetically by steam "cracking" (breaking apart) molecules of naphtha, natural gas liquids, or petroleum.

When ethylene forms a chain:

$$C_2H_4\text{-}C_2H_4\text{-}C_2H_4\text{-}C_2H_4\text{-}C_2H_4\text{-}C_2H_4\text{-}C_2H_4\text{-}C_2H_4\text{-}C_2H_4$$

it becomes polyethylene, which might become a milk jug or a plastic grocery bag.

Whereas ethylene and propylene are considered benign,[1] the monomers styrene, vinyl chloride, and bisphenol A are not. Workers exposed to vinyl chloride suffer disproportionate rates of angiosarcoma of the liver,[2] a cancer that is quite rare in the general population. To make matters worse, vinyl chloride exposure is also associated with a painful condition called band-like acroosteolysis, in which the bones at the tips of the fingers and toes are resorbed, which means that the molecules that make up those bones are repurposed elsewhere in the body.[3] According to the National Toxicology Program, styrene is reasonably anticipated to be a human carcinogen.[4] Exposure may also suppress the immune system,[5] and could even accelerate hearing loss.[6] Studies of Chinese men working in a factory that produced BPA correlated increasing levels of BPA metabolites in their urine with declines in their fertility and libido.[7]

If plastics were just made up of repeating chains of monomers, toxicologists would have a much easier time of it. But the monomer is—literally—only half the story. Up to half the weight of plastics may be additives, fillers, residual catalysts, or accidental byproducts of the reaction.

It can be said of additives, "the secret is in the sauce". We can identify the monomer from the chasing arrows code, but the blend of additives in any particular batch is a trade secret. Manufacturers

---

1. "Ethylene Oxide".

2. Vianna et. al, "Angiosarcoma", 207–10.

3. Freudiger et al., "Acroosteolysis", 216–18; Hahn et al., "Occupational Acroosteolysis", 218–22; Preston et al., "Clinical Aspects", 284–86.

4. "Styrene"

5. Biró, et al., "Lymphocyte Phenotype", 133–40.

6. Hoet and Lison, "Ototoxicity", 127–70.

7. Li et al., "Urine Bisphenol-A", 625–30.

are not required to inform their customers when they change the formulation.

## Common Types of Plastics Additives

Fragrances
Desiccants
Oxygen scavengers
Anti-blocking agents
Anti-static agents
Nucleating agents
Anti-fogging agents
Coupling agents
Lubricants
Mold release agents
Anti-slip agents, slip agents
UV stabilizers
Antimicrobials, biocides
Chemical and physical blowing agents
Additives to control molecular weight
Flame retardants
Adhesives
Fillers and reinforcements
Impact modifiers
Light-sensitizing additives that promote photodegredation
Unintentional additives (residual catalysts and solvents, compounds that migrated in during the polymerization process

Table 2. Intentionally Introduced Components of PVC.[8]

| Monomer | vinyl chloride |
|---|---|
| Stabilizers | cadmium, tin, lead, barium, calcium; alkylphenols such as trisnonylphenolphosphite |
| Plasticizers | diethylhexyl phthalate (DEHP), diisononyl phthalate (DINP), butylbenzyl phthalate (BBP), diisodecyl phthalate (DIDP), di (2-ethylhexyl) adipate (DEHA), organophosphates, trimellitates, epoxidised soybean oil, alkylphenols , tricresyl phosphate (TCP) |
| Antioxidants | bisphenol A (BPA) |
| dyes, tints, and inks | azo-based dyes (diazo, pirazalone, anthraquinone, quiniphthalone, quinoline), lake pigment, carbon black, phthalocyanines, titanium dioxide, lead chromate, cadmium sulfide, hexavalent chromium, mercury |
| flame retardants | bisphenol A (BPA), tetrabromobisphenol A (TBBPA), other polybrominated compounds, tricresyl phosphate (TCP) |
| antimicrobials | triclosan, 2-n-octyl-4 isothiazolin-3, copper-8-quinoleate, nano-scale silver |
| UV stabilizers | carbon black, hydrobenzophenone, phenolic benzotriazoles (UV-320, UV-326, UV-327, UV-328) |
| impact modifiers | (no publicly available information readily accessible) |
| anti-fogging agents | ethyloxylates of nonylphenols |
| anti-static agents | alkyl quaternary ammonium salts, alkyl phosphonium, alkyl sulfonium salts, dithiocarbamic acid |
| anti-blocking agents | talc, diatomaceous earth, silica |
| mold release agents | (no publicly available information readily accessible) |
| fillers and reinforcements | clay, silica, talc, wood flour |
| Lubricants | metallic soaps |
| oxygen scavengers | copper loaded/ascorbate loaded silica |

8. The addition of antimicrobials is not because the monomer itself is at risk of microbial attack (i.e., it does not biodegrade); however, some of the additives are. For this reason, and as a selling point for consumers who are concerned about bacterial contamination of the products stored in PVC containers and wraps, antimicrobials are introduced.

In 1987, Ana Soto and Carlos Sonnenschein at Tufts University were performing experiments on estrogen-sensitive breast cancer cells, testing under which conditions they multiplied (in the presence of the hormone estrogen), and under what conditions they did not (in the absence of estrogen). Suddenly, both the control and the experimental cells began wildly proliferating. They assumed that they had made a mistake and contaminated their lab, so they absorbed the expense of throwing that batch away and starting over. But again, the untreated cells proliferated as though they were in the presence of estrogen.[9]

The researchers suspected that the problem was with the test tubes, but the manufacturer at first refused to answer their questions. After a great deal of wasted time and lab supplies, they discovered that the culprit was an estrogen mimic, nonylphenol, that had been added to their polystyrene test tubes. Corning had been receiving complaints that their centrifuge tubes were brittle. In response, they tinkered with the chemical composition of the tubes. They did not notify their customers. This of course raised concerns for the researchers. Could nonylphenol cause the same sort of breast cancer cell proliferation in humans that it could *in vitro*?

However, nonylphenol continues to be a common additive in polystyrene and in PVC—even in products intended for use in food processing and food packaging. Alkylphenols (the broad class of chemicals that includes nonylphenols) leach into water that flows through PVC tubing. Some polyethylene is also manufactured with alkylphenols. The breakdown products of the spermicide nonoxynyl-9 include nonylphenol, which is thought to be taken up by the permeable mucus membrane of the vagina.[10] Yet, unlike the now commonplace "BPA-free" labels, we do not see products labeled "alkylphenol-free".

History has a way of repeating itself. In 2008, while trying to develop drugs to treat Parkinson's disease, Andrew Holt and his team had been using ammonium chloride to inhibit the activity of

9. Soto et al., "P-Nonylphenol", 167–73.
10. "Endocrine Disruptors".

the *c-Abl* enzyme in brain cells. However, the polypropylene tubes that they used to transfer liquids were leaching oleamide and quaternary ammonium, which, as it turns out, were not only biologically active but were toxic to the brain cells in their petri dishes.[11] Just like ethylene, oleamide comes in natural and synthetic forms. A natural version of oleamide is found in the cerebrospinal fluid of sleep-deprived animals, including humans. This endogenous oleamide induces sleep, part of a negative feedback loop. A synthetic version is used as an additive in polyvinyl chloride, low-density polyethylene, and polypropylene, where it is intended to function as a slip agent, a lubricant, or a corrosion inhibitor. Quaternary amines (known as "quats" for short) are synthetic neurotoxic biocides. Yet we continue to consume yogurt from polypropylene tubs, blissfully ignorant of whether these were added to each batch of polypropylene.

We are told, of course, that none of *our* exposures are dangerous, because the amounts we come into contact with are far below regulatory thresholds. However, as we will see in the following section, the dose does not always make the poison.

## TEACHING ABOUT ENDOCRINE DISRUPTION AND LOW-DOSE TOXICOLOGY USING THE STORY OF PLASTICS

> "It is very nice to drink milk at an unsegregated lunch counter—but not when there's strontium-90 in it."
> —Rev. Dr. Martin Luther King, Jr.[12]

> "For many people, the lived experience of police violence and toxic exposure—these different forms of physical vulnerability—both live together. We have to think of

---

11. McDonald et al., "Bioactive Contaminants", 917; Mittelstaedt, "Researchers Raise Alarm";
Olivieri et al., "On the Disruption", 697–703.

12. Dellinger "Dr. King's Interconnected".

them together instead of thinking of them separately."
—Lindsey Dillon[13]

My doctoral studies stalled, and nearly fizzled out completely, while I struggled to justify to myself where I was spending my time and attention. While I was busy memorizing the molecular structures of polymers, nine members of a Bible study group at Emanuel African Methodist Episcopal Church were murdered for no other reason than the color of their skin. One day that summer, a Black trans friend apologized to me for using a plastic fork. I remember my fury: "Until you can walk down the street in safety, I don't give a *f\*ck* what fork you use." I don't pretend that this tension is resolved, but I have found that my study of plastics might be useful, after all, in making the case that toxics are a civil rights issue.

We poison ourselves, and each other, in so many ways. Our dependence on plastics is just one of those ways. The lives of people pushed to the margins of society are sometimes taken quickly with guns and sometimes taken slowly with poisons.

Toxicology, as its name suggests, is the study of toxic chemicals: the effects that they may have on living organisms. This information is helpful in understanding and mitigating the risks that these substances pose. We will first examine one of the most basic tenants of the discipline, piece by piece.

## 1. Risk = Hazard × **Exposure**

Is exposure a choice? If so, is it a choice at the individual or the societal level?

The first principle of toxicology is that in order for something to harm us, it must first find its way into our body. Much of risk management and quantitative risk assessment focus on estimating how much of a given substance we might come into contact with in various scenarios. These tools of analysis are much less useful when a substance is as ubiquitous as plastic.

---

13. Mock, "How Environmental Injustice".

Plastics are everywhere in the environment. Pieces of polystyrene have been found on remote ice floes in the Arctic Ocean,[14] microplastic fibers litter seafloor sediment,[15] and tiny plastic particles are even in the air that we breathe (both indoors and outdoors).[16] Even the steam rising from manhole covers may be a source of styrene particles.[17] A toxicologist would not be concerned about any of this, until they were convinced that these plastics are also in our bodies.

The line of demarcation between our body and "the environment" is not as clear a boundary as we might expect. Some toxicologists make the case that plastics pass through our digestive system without being absorbed, and therefore technically remain outside the body. There are plastics that are tiny enough, however, that they can take the same path that nutrients do. Tiny PVC particles, between five and one hundred microns, which are roughly the size of milled corn, pass easily through the gut into the bloodstream.[18] (By comparison, the threads comprising a spider's web are two to three microns thick, and a human hair roughly six hundred microns.) From the digestive tract, they enter the circulatory system, and may eventually make their way into the cerebrospinal fluid, even crossing the blood-brain barrier.[19] Nanoscale polystyrene beads cross the placenta.[20]

Most of the research along this line has been conducted by scientists in the employ of the pharmaceutical industry. This property of plastics is regularly exploited in order to deliver the active ingredients of our medications to their target organ before being metabolized.[21] In 2004, a young man in the Boston area sought help at a fertility clinic because he and his wife were having dif-

14. Doward, "How Did That Get There?"

15. Ling et al., "Ubiquity of Microplastics", 104–10.

16. Gasperi et al., "First Overview".

17. Teimouri Sendesi et al., "Worksite Chemical", 325–33.

18. Volkheimer, "Hematogenous Dissemination", 164–71.

19. Mattson et al., "Brain Damage", 11452.

20. Wick et al. , "Barrier Capacity", 432.

21. Hussain et al., "Recent Advances", 107–42.

ficulty conceiving. When his urine was tested, doctors discovered seventeen thousand parts per billion of dibutyl phthalate. That's one hundred times more dibutyl phthalate than had ever been recorded before in a human being at that time, and double what the US Environmental Protection Agency has deemed safe.[22] The source: Asacol, a Food and Drug Administration-approved time-release medication that he had been taking as prescribed for an inflamed colon. The enteric coating contains dibutyl phthalate. So do the coatings of the drugs didanosine, omeprazole, and theophylline, among others.[23]

This encapsulation technology is used not only to deliver medications, but also vitamins.[24] Polyethylene, polyamide (nylon), polyvinylpyrrolidone, polymethacrylate—among other natural and synthetic materials—may be used to manufacture "nutriceutical beadlets" that are added to food to enhance its nutritional profile.

Plastics are ubiquitous in our food as well as in our medications.[25] Some polymers are direct additives and others indirect additives (Table 3). Many are used in food processing in ways that are invisible to consumers and are not disclosed on food labels. For example, ion-exchange membranes consisting of polyethylene, polystyrene, and/or perfluorinated compounds are used to filter grapefruit juice and to purify water.[26]

Table 3. US Food and Drug Administration-approved Polymeric Additives in Food.[27]

22. Cone, "Prescription Drugs".

23. Betts, "Phthalates in Prescription Drugs", A74.

24. Moskin, "Superfood or Monster".

25. EFSA Contam Panel, "Statement", 4501–31.

26. "CFR".

27. Information in table compiled from FDA Code of Federal Regulations (see "CFR").

| Polymer | Purpose |
|---|---|
| vinyl chloride-vinylidene chloride copolymer | a component of coating on fresh citrus fruits |
| polyvinyl acetate, polyethylene, poly styrene – butadiene rubber, butyl rubber, and/or polyisobutylene. | permissible components of chewing gum |
| polyethylene | a replacement for roughage in feedlot rations for finishing slaughter cattle, or as a protective coating for fresh avocados, bananas, beets, coconuts, eggplant, garlic, grapefruit, lemons, limes, mango, muskmelons, onions, oranges, papaya, peas (in pods), pineapple, plantain, pumpkin, rutabaga, squash (acorn), sweet potatoes, tangerines, turnips, watermelon, Brazil nuts, chestnuts, filberts, hazelnuts, pecans, and walnuts (all nuts in shells) |
| polypropylene glycol, polyethylene glycol | defoaming agents used in beet sugar and yeast |
| acrilonitrile copolymers and polyacrylamide | as a flocculent in the clarification of beet sugar juice and liquor or cane sugar juice and liquor or corn starch hydrolyzate |
| methacrylic acid-divinyl benzene copolymer | a carrier for vitamin $B_{12}$ in nutritional supplements |
| polyacrylamide | the coating in gelatin capsules |

| copolymer condensates of ethylene oxide and propylene oxide | as a solubilizing and stabilizing agent in flavor concentrates, in scald baths for poultry defeathering, as a foam control and rinse adjuvant in hog dehairing machine, or as a dough conditioner in yeast-leavened bakery products |
|---|---|
| polyvinyl acetate | a diluent for color additive mixtures for drug use |
| Polyvinylpyrrolidone poly(2-vinylpyridine-co-styrene) | a coating for cattle feed |

Plastics used in food packaging are considered *indirect* additives. Tea bags are often made of plastic.[28] Even bottled water that is sold in glass may be contaminated with chemicals that leached from the plastic processing equipment in the factory.[29]

In the animal husbandry literature, we find a warning that boar semen samples packaged in a multilayer plastic bag resulted in "high levels of reproductive failure".[30] The suspected culprit is the polyurethane adhesive between the layers of the bag. The adhesive contained octyl phthalate, 13-docosenamide (erucamide), and bisphenol A diglycidyl ether (BADGE) as well as two unknown compounds that appeared to be cyclic phthalates. The authors note that, "boar spermatozoa are frequently used as biosensors for detecting toxic substances."[31] This is of interest to public health because similar materials are used for packaging food for human consumption.[32]

"Plasticulture" (the use of plastic in agriculture) may constitute another type of indirect plastic contamination. Microplastics may be added to soil to promote aeration (alternatively, earthworms could be recruited for this purpose). Some growers now

28. Orci, "Are Tea Bags".
29. Wagner and Oehlmann, "Endocrine Disruptors", 278–86.
30. Nerin et al., "Compounds".
31. Andersson et al., "Boar Spermatozoa", 2041–52.
32. "Cross-linked Polyurethanes".

use artificial soil, which may be a blend of gel-coated "foam plastic fragments" or "thermoplastic resin foamed particles".[33] Some growers steam their soil before planting. One paper notes that this causes the polystyrene in artificial or enhanced soil to melt to 10 percent of its original volume and recommends that the soil be steamed prior to mixing in the plastic.[34] Studies have demonstrated that heat accelerates the leaching of toxicants from plastics, but to my knowledge, no studies have been conducted to determine what leaches into soil from steamed polystyrene fragments.[35]

Irrigation pipes, pond liners, and many other pieces of the agricultural infrastructure rely on plastics. Thin polyethylene sheets, used as mulch to prevent weeds from sprouting, cover forty-nine million acres of agricultural land in China.[36] In the United States, 130,000 tons of mulch film were used in 2004, and that number has been rising every year.[37] Some of this may be reused from season to season, while other types are designed to disintegrate.[38] However, the pieces are no less toxic than they were before disintegration; they are merely smaller and easier to ingest, and have an increased surface area to potentially adsorb lipophilic contaminants, such as pesticides.

Not all of the plastics in foods are there legally. In China, some unscrupulous manufacturers of baby formula and milk were found to be watering down their products and then spiking them

33. Mankiewicz, "Artificial Soil"; Suzuki and Azuma, "Artificial Soil".

34. Matkin, "Perlite".

35. Endocrine disruption happens in plants as well, because hormonal signaling is conserved across species. Our estrogen receptors respond to the hormonal signals that plants send (phytoestrogens), and likewise, plants are affected by the pharmaceutical and industrial estrogens that we release into their environment. BPA, for example, interferes with the communication between rhizobial bacteria and the host plant, which can inhibit their ability to fix nitrogen. This raises the question of whether this alters the plants' nutritional composition, or whether any of the contaminants are taken up into the parts of plants that are used for food.

36. Shuping and Wills, "Plastic Film".

37. Kasirajan and Ngouajio, "Polyethylene", 501–29.

38. Ibid.

with melamine, which served to blind the quality assurance tests to the low levels of natural proteins. However, melamine does not function in the body as a natural protein would. Instead, it tends to cause kidney disease.

Some vendors describe openly how they increase their profit margins by passing off ersatz eggs.[39] While melted plastic is still a thick liquid, before it cools and hardens, they mix it with starch, coagulant, pigments, sodium alginate (a derivative of brown algae), paraffin wax, gypsum powder and calcium carbonate. The final product has a realistic-looking shell that cracks open to reveal what appears to be a typical yolk and egg white. The key to detection, consumers are told, is that a plastic egg yolk quickly breaks. Sadly, this is not a reliable screening tool because many real egg yolks do this, too.

Rice is another target of entrepreneurial ingenuity.[40] A video demonstrates the process of extruding sheets of polyethylene to resemble grains of rice. The plastic "rice" is mixed with actual rice (to make it harder to detect) and exported. The author warns that, at this time, neither government inspectors nor consumers have any way to distinguish the counterfeit from the real rice.

Unintentional contamination is yet another problem. Researchers found microplastic contamination in all of the samples of beer that they analyzed,[41] which they speculate may have been shed from workers' synthetic clothing. Another possibility is that the process used tap water that was already contaminated. A recent study supports this, finding plastic fibers in over 80 percent of tap water samples taken from five continents.[42] Honey,[43] sea salt, lake salt, and rock salt[44] sold in supermarkets have been found to be contaminated with microplastics, including fibers of polyethylene

39. Boehler, "Bad Eggs".

40. Ayitey, "Rice Producers".

41. Liebezeit and Liebezeit, "Synthetic Particles", 1574–78.

42. Tyree and Morrison, "Invisibles".

43. Liebezeit and Liebezeit, "Non-pollen Particulates"; Mühlschlegel et al., "Lack of Evidence", 1982–89.

44. Yang et al., "Microplastic Pollution", 13622–27.

terephthalate (the plastic used to make disposable water bottles and fleece), polyethylene (which is used to make plastic shopping bags), and cellophane (a bio-based plastic film).

### Avoiding Exposure: Case Study No. 1

BPA was originally designed to be a medicinal synthetic estrogen, although it was never marketed for that purpose. Its prototype spent decades on a shelf, this history largely forgotten, until chemists polymerized it and rescued it from obscurity. The resulting polycarbonate became a popular substitute for glass in everything from food packaging to corrective lenses to labware.

The estrogenic property of BPA was accidentally rediscovered in 1993 when researchers at Stanford University noticed that something in their plastic lab equipment was causing all of their yeast-based estrogenicity assays to come out positive—even the negative controls. It turns out that this effect increased after they put their polycarbonate flasks in an autoclave, which exposed them to high heat and pressure.[45]

In 1998, Patricia Hunt was exploring the causes of meiotic aneuploidy (an incorrect number of chromosomes caused by errors during meiosis) in female mice. A technician in her lab used a highly alkaline detergent to wash the cages and water bottles. The polycarbonate was damaged, and the bonds between the links in the chains of BPA weakened. Bits of free BPA broke away from the chains and into the mice's drinking water.[46] Although at the time is was not known, BPA is also absorbed through the skin of mammals.[47] Perhaps some of the BPA transferred from the plastic cages into the bloodstream of the mice as they rubbed against the walls of their enclosures to scratch an itch or relieve boredom. The

---

45. Krishnan et al., "Bisphenol-A", 2279–86.

46. Hunt et al., "Bisphenol A Exposure", 546–53.

47. Zalko et al.,"Viable Skin", 424–30.

rates of chromosomal abnormalities in the eggs of exposed mice jumped from one to two percent to around 40 percent.[48]

After Patricia Hunt and her colleagues published their story, a flurry of research followed. Le et al. established that "Bisphenol A *is* released from polycarbonate drinking bottles and mimics the neurotoxic actions of estrogen in developing cerebellar neurons."[49] Sandra Biedermann-Brem found that even baby bottles washed at home in the dishwasher leached BPA, although controversy ensued as to whether these amounts were high enough to warrant concern.[50] Oberlies et al. found that the presence of certain microbes on the surface of polycarbonate increased the rate of leaching.[51] Viñas et al. looked into techniques for measuring trace levels of BPA migration from the lining of food cans,[52] while Mercea analyzed the physical and chemical conditions under which leaching was maximized. As expected, heat and extreme pH (as well as ozone) promoted leaching.[53]

If BPA was leaching, how much was finding its way into people's bodies?

Mariscal-Arcas et al. measured BPA in the urine of pregnant women in Spain, which correlated positively with their use of canned foods.[54] Von Goetz et al. found that the use of canned food and polycarbonate baby bottles increased BPA levels in consumers.[55] Researchers at the Silent Spring Institute in Newton, Massachusetts decided to test this. They found five families willing to eat exclusively fresh foods without any plastic packaging for three days. The levels of BPA in the participants' urine samples decreased significantly (but did not completely disappear) during the inter-

48. Cohen, "Plastics Ingredient".

49. Le et al., "Bisphenol A", 149–56.

50. Biedermann-Brem et al., "Release", 1053–60; Simoneau et al., "Comparison", 1763–68.

51. Oberlies et al., "Microbial-mediated", 271–75.

52. Viñas et al, "Comparison", 115–25.

53. Mercea, "Physicochemical", 579–53.

54. Mariscal-Arcas et al., "Dietary Exposure", 506–10.

55. Von Goetz et al., "Bisphenol A", 473–87.

vention, and then returned to pre-intervention levels when the families resumed eating packaged foods.[56] Soon, however, another route of exposure to BPA took center stage: we are absorbing BPA each time we touch cash register receipts.[57]

BPA has since been linked to a wide variety of ill effects in both humans and lab animals. These range from metabolic syndrome, obesity, heart and liver disease, breast cancer, early onset of puberty, attention deficit hyperactivity disorder (ADHD), and infertility, to increased susceptibility to methamphetamine addiction and diminished maternal instincts. A series of studies in a cohort of Chinese factory workers measured their exposure to BPA in the workplace and the levels of BPA metabolites in their urine (to see how much of what they were touching and breathing was being absorbed by their bodies). Not surprisingly, there was a direct correlation. The researchers also took semen samples and asked the men to fill out extensive questionnaires about their reproductive health. Men's fertility and libido decline as their levels of BPA rise. The men with the highest levels have two to four times the risk of poor semen quality.[58]

The strength of evidence for each of these claims varies, but many consumers would like to take a precautionary approach and opt for "BPA-free." However, often manufacturers will neither confirm nor deny that their plastic contains endocrine disrupting compounds. In other cases, information is provided, but in code.

As mentioned previously, the resin code (a number from one to seven in a triangle of chasing arrows) stamped on the bottom of commodity plastic items indicates which monomer (chemical building block) was linked into long repeated chains to form that plastic. It may be vinyl chloride ("3"), styrene ("6"), or propylene ("5"), or it might be one of several ethylene-based plastics ("1", "2", or "4"). Some may wish to avoid vinyl chloride and styrene as well because of the health risks that their manufacture entails for the workers, or out of concern that the residual monomer could leach

56. Rudell, et al. "Food Packaging", 914–20.

57. Braun et al., "Variability", 131.

58. Li et al., "Urine Bisphenol-A", 625–30.

and expose them. Our hypothetical BPA-averse shopper would know that resin code "7", however, simply translates as "other," a catch-all category that includes not only BPA-based polycarbonate but also bio-based plastics such as polylactic acid (PLA). Other uses of BPA, such as thermal receipt paper and the epoxy lining of food and beverage cans and even on the underside of lids for glass jars, are not labeled. Even when not used as the monomer, BPA might make an appearance as an additive, either in its plain form, or joined to a bromine (TBBPA, or tetrabromobisphenol A). It is intended to act as a flame retardant in various plastics, most often in PVC. Thus, a product that is not polycarbonate may contain BPA anyway, if it was used as an additive.

BPA has even been found in fresh produce grown in a green-house built with polycarbonate panels that may have off-gassed BPA when exposed to direct sunlight for prolonged periods.[59] Eight out of fourteen fresh vegetables on an Italian farm, for example, contained 250–1000 nanograms per gram of BPA even though the food had not had any direct contact with plastic.[60] One author reported, "The amount of BPA found in fresh food was ... in the same range as potential migration levels from microwaving polycarbonate containers. What is significant is the indication that even fresh food that had no direct contact with BPA may still contain it."[61]

To complicate matters further, products marked "BPA-free" may contain BPA's first cousin, bisphenol S (BPS). BPS is not as well-studied as BPA, but from the research that has been done, it does not appear to be any safer.[62]

Consumer demand is pushing for increased transparency. As one response, George Bittner, a professor of neuroscience at the University of Texas, Austin, founded a lab that has begun screening plastics for estrogenic activity (EA) for a fee, allowing companies

---

59. "Blissfully Unaware".
60. Vivacqua et al., "Food Contaminants", 275–84.
61. "Blissfully Unaware".
62. Rochester and Bolden, "Bisphenol S", 643.

to label their products as "free of estrogenic activity."[63] While this is certainly valuable information, we cannot conclude that a plastic is safe because of the absence of EA. It could still have androgenic activity (meaning that it could interfere with testosterone signaling). It could still interfere with insulin, thyroid hormones, or any number of other signaling mechanisms in the body.

## QUESTIONS FOR DISCUSSION

Do market-based solutions, such as Bittner's lab's services and the proliferation of BPA-free plastics that substitute one toxicant for another, adequately protect consumers, or do they provide a sense of false security (for private profit)? Could the market be better regulated to achieve consumer protection? Or do solutions lie outside the market?

## *Avoiding Exposure: Case Study No. 2*

The late Dr. Earle Bartley of the Department of Animal Sciences at Kansas State University experimented with plastic cattle feed. His first mixture was 80 to 90 percent polyethylene and 10 to 20 percent polypropylene. One problem with the prototype was that the cows could detect it and consistently chose to eat around it. He reportedly attributed the cows' "avoidance behavior" to the slippery quality of the plastic. After he changed the shape of the pellets, he had more luck. Instead of eating four pounds of hay a day, his cows ate one-tenth of a pound of plastic, at a considerable cost savings. The indigestible but thoroughly masticated shreds of plastic floated at the top of the cows' rumens. Carbon-14 tracing did not detect any of the plastic itself in the cows' bloodstream. At slaughter, he boasted that "about twenty pounds" of the pellet shreds could be "recovered, melted, recycled, and reintroduced

63. Bilbrey, "BPA-Free".

into another animal."[64] The license for this work was transferred to Ralston-Purina by Exxon, which had provided funding.

Other researchers have tried feeding livestock various forms of polyethylene pellets[65] and polypropylene ribbons.[66] Some hit upon an even cheaper solution: implant regular plastic sponges and "pot scrubbers"[67] directly into the cows' stomachs. As the sponges and scrubbers absorb liquid and expand, they create a feeling of fullness and save on feed costs, perhaps reducing greenhouse gas emissions as well.[68] Whetsell, Prigge, and Nestor published a paper explaining that when they filled a cow's rumen with seventy-five tennis balls, the cow's appetite decreased.[69]

Although it is unclear how widespread the use of plastic in cattle feed is, ongoing use of polyethylene cattle feed was mentioned in the public health literature as recently as 2007,[70] and as the article describes, this is but one example among many questionable practices in industrial feedlots.

## QUESTIONS FOR DISCUSSION

How would a consumer who eats meat source animals raised without plastic roughage? What constraints might limit consumers' choices?

## Avoiding Exposure: Case Study No. 3

A two-pound premature infant receiving standard care in the neonatal intensive care unit (NICU) absorbs as much as 160,000 times more DEHP (one type of phthalate, a plasticizer used to make PVC

64. Schell, *Modern Meat*.

65. Welch, "Physical Parameters", 2750–54.

66. White and Reynolds, "Various Sources", 705–10.

67. Loerch, "Efficacy", 2321–28.

68. Christophersen et al., "In vitro Methane", 384–89.

69. Whetsell et al., "Influence", 1806–17.

70. Sapkota et al., "What Do We Feed", 663–70.

flexible) than is considered safe for the liver.[71] DEHP is a known endocrine disruptor and probable carcinogen.[72] Polyvinyl chloride is used to make IV tubing, blood bags, oxygen cannulas, umbilical vessel catheters, peripherally inserted central catheter (PICC) lines, and a variety of other medical equipment.[73] It is also commonly used in homes and hospitals as flooring, shower curtains, and windows. How does healthcare differ from other types of consumer purchases? How would you regulate medical exposures to plastics?

## Questions for Discussion

1. Given that plastics are ubiquitous and often invisible, how can consumers avoid exposure? Are public health messages such as "avoid microwaving food in plastic" and "avoid washing plastic kitchenware in hot water or in harsh detergents" helpful or harmful? (Do they give consumers who follow them a false sense of security that they can eliminate or limit their exposure through individual behavioral changes alone, without structural/regulatory changes?)

2. What regulatory measures (requiring labeling, enacting bans) are called for? Are the regulatory measures already in place working? Why or why not? Use the FDA rules on food additives as a place to start.

3. Is a focus on "consumers" sufficiently protective? Whose exposures would be unaddressed by these measures?

## 2. Risk = **Hazard** × Exposure

The potential of a substance to harm a living organism was thought to be largely a function of the dose, and of how it moves through

71. Mallow and Fox, "Phthalates", 892–97.
72. "ToxFAQs".
73. "PVC and DEHP".

the body (this is referred to as toxicokinetics). Substances that are persistent and bioaccumulative were thought to be more dangerous than substances that the body could quickly break down and excrete. Endocrine disruptors challenge both of these assumptions.

Hormones act as messengers. Think of Pheidippides, the courier who ran nearly twenty-six miles from Marathon to Athens to deliver news of the Greek victory against the Persians. The poor lad delivered his message, "Rejoice! Victory is ours!" with his last breath. Though he did not live to see it, his words set events in motion that, according to the poets, shaped the history of the Western world.

Once a message has been delivered (or an alarm silenced), the story is just beginning. So with our hormones. BPA, the chemical we discussed above, has a half-life of less than six hours.[74] However, within that brief time of residency in the body, it can send messages that will have long-lasting repercussions, possibly for generations to come.

These messengers may impersonate or thwart natural signals to the brain, pancreas, or adrenal glands, in addition to estrogen, androgen, and thyroid hormones. These signals can disrupt reproductive development, interfere with appetite regulation, shift metabolism, and much more.

## Lag Time

One of the nine principles for determining causality in public health research that epidemiologist Bradford Hill articulated in 1965 is that exposure precedes effect.[75] The more consistently and the sooner the effect follows the cause, the easier it is for observers to make the connection. When Morgan Spurlock decided to eat nothing but McDonald's for one month, he consumed twice the

---

74. "Bisphenol A Metabolism".
75. Fedak et al., "Applying", 14.

recommended calories for his size and activity level, and he suffered an immediate and visible decline in his health.[76]

It is well-established that certain medications, such as some anti-depressants and anti-seizure drugs, cause weight gain. When we perceive an increase in body mass soon after the patient begins taking the medication, attributing the effect to the cause is a relatively simple matter. The patient can be queried to find out if their appetite has increased, or if they are feeling lethargic and getting less exercise. Laboratory studies can be designed to determine by which pathway the drug is affecting weight, and in some cases the pharmaceutical researchers can tweak the design of their molecule to prevent this side effect.

With environmental endocrine disruptors, however, the lag time may be so long that we do not make the connection. Our metabolism seems to be most vulnerable to obesogenic insults before birth. The Developmental Origins of Health and Disease hypothesis has described how children born to women who endured starvation while pregnant during the "Hunger Winter" in Holland, though underweight at birth, tended to become obese adults.[77] Similarly, mice exposed to the synthetic estrogen diethylstilbestrol in utero grew to be two or three times the size of their unexposed peers, despite being fed the same number of calories.[78]

In the same way that we don't necessarily see an immediate adverse effect after an exposure to an endocrine disrupting contaminant (EDC), we also don't necessarily see an immediate improvement in a person's health after a reduction in EDC exposure. Thus, the pseudo-scientific diet books that I have seen that encourage readers to reduce their contact with certain chemicals in order to see short-term weight loss are bound to fail. The reason for this can be understood through a metaphor. If a mail carrier delivers a letter with bad news, you won't return to your previous emotional state once the U.S. Postal Service truck has driven away. You might have read the letter and begun taking action to mitigate

76. *Supersize Me!*
77. Schulz, "Dutch Hunger", 16757–58.
78. Newbold et al., "Developmental Exposure", 478–80.

the situation. In the same way, hormones are the body's messengers. Once they have delivered their news, they set into motion a chain of events that will continue whether or not the hormone (or hormone mimic) disappears.

## Mixture Effects

No one is exposed to only one toxicant at a time. Scientists now speak of the "exposome"—the universe of physical, chemical, and biological conditions that an individual encounters.[79] To give a simple example, the obesogenic endocrine disruptor BPA can be absorbed through the skin. Touching a thermal receipt is one way that we come into contact with BPA (or, more frequently now, the related compound BPS). A person who has just applied a hand lotion is likely to absorb more BPA than someone whose skin is dry, because the dermal penetration-enhancing ingredients in the lotion not only allow the body to absorb more moisturizer, but also more BPA. Since we are, for the most part, unaware of what we are exposed to (let alone able to quantify these exposures), we have no way to untangle the web of connections among them.

## Individual Variations in Susceptibility

Scientists are trained to look for consistency. This makes sense, of course, on an intuitive level. We do this, too, when we look for exceptions to the rule to justify our risk-taking. I've heard people use anecdotes like, "My grandfather smoked for sixty years and he didn't get lung cancer. He lived to a ripe old age!" to downplay the very real harm that smoking causes. Not only is it true that each person has a unique set of exposures, it is also true that each person responds differently.

Imagine we could create a computer program that could model not just risk for a population, but for you as an individual. Let's pretend we could make it cost-effective to type your complete

79. "Exposome".

genome (the genes with which you were born), epigenome (the pattern of expression of these genes), and the microbiome (the community of tiny organisms that colonize our bodies and which perform a variety of life-sustaining functions). Then, let's pretend that we know what you were exposed to from conception until this moment—the precise doses and timing. And let's imagine that we had psychometric data on your mental and emotional health. This sort of information would be necessary to claim that you are making informed choices about your health.

Widely accepted ways to boost resilience include nutritional interventions. Having an adequate calcium and iron intake, for example, reduces the amount of lead that is absorbed by the body.[80] What this means is that when we are lonely and depressed, we are more vulnerable to a toxic exposure than when we are feeling connected to others and optimistic about our future. Research suggests that laughter really is medicinal,[81] and that the chemicals our bodies make after an orgasm can boost our immune function.[82]

Individual variations in susceptibility mean not only that risk varies from person to person, but that even the risk for a given individual changes over time. Vulnerability is at its peak during prenatal development and in early childhood, falls after adolescence, and then rises again somewhat in the twilight years. Even over the course of a day, the impact an exposure has will vary. For example, a medication given in the morning might have very different effects on the body than it would if the same dose were taken at night. We are learning that interrupting the light-dark cycle (particularly with exposure to blue light at night) adversely affects our body's metabolism, even altering the detoxification enzymes that our liver produces.[83] Disruption of the circadian rhythm has been linked to an increased risk of diabetes, obesity, and certain types of cancer, among other problems.

---

80. Klauder and Petering, "Protective Value", 77–80.

81. Bennett and Lengacher, "Humor", 159–64.

82. Ellison Rodgers, *Sex*.

83. Sharma et al., "Circadian", 191–213.

Adding another layer of complexity to the issue of risk and individual susceptibility, researchers in the emerging interdisciplinary field of conservation medicine (also known as Planetary Health or One Health) have begun documenting an increasing body burden of contaminants alongside an extraordinary rise in the rate of obesity[84] and cancer[85] in wild animals that live in proximity to humans, including captive animals (those in zoos and aquariums). For that matter, the age at onset of sexual maturity in some whales is falling. In humans, early puberty is often attributed to increased body mass.[86] It is difficult to blame these epidemics on "poor lifestyle choices" on the part of wildlife. They are hardly sedentary—those that are probably don't last long before being subsumed into the food web. They do not smoke, nor do they imbibe. They are not swayed by junk food advertisements nor do they crave soda, as far as we know. All this casts doubt on the importance of "healthy behaviors" and the victim-blaming (human) public health dogma that currently dominates policy discussions.

## Route of Exposure and Type of Dose

Dose is not just about how much of a substance the body takes in, but the timing of the delivery. For example, the medicine Lupron, given once a month, halts puberty that has begun too soon. The chemical composition of the drug, however, is nearly identical to the natural hormones that the body secretes in hourly pulses to *start* puberty.

For some substances, the route of exposure matters. Mercury, an example we will come back to in much more detail in a later section, provides a great illustration of this principle. Elemental mercury—the silver goo that children used to play with when an old-fashioned thermometer broke—is unlikely to cause serious

---

84. Klimentidis, "Canaries", 1626–1632.
85. McAloose and Newton, "Wildlife", 518–526.
86. Brown and Lockyer, "Whales", 717–81.

acute harm when touched or even when swallowed. However, if it is inhaled, it is quite dangerous.

It isn't always obvious how a particular chemical is entering our body. I remember a real estate agent responding dismissively to my questions about lead paint, "Well, you aren't planning to eat it, are you?" There are adults who eat paint chips (*pica* is the term for a craving for substances that are not generally considered food, such as dirt or chalk or ice). What is in the dust that we unwittingly eat all the time? Researchers from the Silent Spring Institute tested household dust and found up to forty-five toxic chemicals, ten of which were present in at least 90 percent of their samples.[87] What is known as hand-to-mouth behavior (a behavior at which toddlers excel)?

A chemical spill in West Virginia contaminated a river with crude 4-methylcyclohexanemethanol. Risk assessments showed that people should be safe at the levels at which they were exposed by drinking their tap water. However, many people were reporting symptoms. They mystery was solved when the risk assessors realized that they had forgotten to account for the fact that people were also *breathing* a volatilized form of the chemical, and absorbing it through their skin, when they showered.

When dieticians evaluate food intake, they do not account for the polyfluoroalkyl phosphate esters from the wrapping "paper" that migrates into food or the BPA that leaches into soft drinks from the lining of the cans, depending on the pH of the foodstuff, on the temperature at which it was packaged and stored, its exposure to sunlight, time, and so many other factors. Our risk assessments are incomplete.

## Case Study: Unanticipated Environmental Interactions

Trenbolone acetate, a synthetic anabolic steroid, is used to make cattle gain weight more quickly. Though banned in the EU, this drug is administered to over twenty million cattle a year in the

---

87. Mitro et al., "Consumer", 10661–72.

United States. They metabolize and excrete it as 17α-trenbolone. Because 17α-trenbolone can harm fish at very low doses, scientists wanted to understand what happens when the manure of treated cows enters streams. When they sampled the streams during the day, they found that the 17α-trenbolone quickly broke down in sunlight. They thought that was the end of the story, packed up, and went home. In 2013, however, researchers from the University of Iowa accidentally discovered that at night, the molecular pieces were reassembling themselves.[88] It turns out that other chemicals with a similar structure can perform the same trick, with the rate of reassembly determined in part by the pH and temperature of the water.

Other unanticipated environmental interactions can lead to unexpected risks. For example, when ozone touches human skin, it reacts with squalene (an oily antioxidant that protects our skin from chemical damage) to form volatile compounds, one of which is 4-oxopentanal.[89] 4-Oxopentanal bears an unfortunate structural similarity to diacetyl, a component of artificial butter flavor. It doesn't seem to be a problem when we eat it, but inhaling enough of its seductive, buttery aroma can cause irreversible lung damage. The condition, bronchiolitis obliterans, is now commonly referred to as "popcorn lung," named for the highly exposed workers in the flavor mixing room of a Jasper, Missouri, popcorn plant whose misfortune lead to its discovery.[90]

Even the most sophisticated computers could not begin to predict all of the possible interactions of even one compound with all of the other natural and synthetic substances it could encounter in the environment, and the "uncertainty factors" assigned in quantitative risk assessments underestimate our knowledge gaps.

88. Peplow, "Hormone Disruptors".
89. Biello, "Indoor Air".
90. "Flavorings-related".

## Case Study: Chemical Mixtures in Sarnia

The twelve-square-kilometer (4.6-square-mile) Sarnia 45 Indian Reserve, home of the Aamjiwnaang (Chippewa) First Nation, is located on the banks of the St. Clair River, near Lake Huron in the province of Ontario. The area was designated by treaty as a reservation in 1827.[91] In 1858, settlers realized that the substance that the Aamjiwnaang people had long been using to waterproof their canoes was oil. First the settlers eagerly exploited the gum beds, and then thirty-eight kilometers (twenty-five miles) south-east, drilled North America's first oil wells. Towns with names like Petrolia and Oil City grew rapidly. Soon after, companies that use oil as a feedstock moved in, and Sarnia and the surrounding land became known as Chemical Valley. Today, approximately 40 percent of Canada's chemical industry, including over sixty plastics and pesticide manufacturers and petrochemical refineries, surround the Aamjiwnaang.[92]

All of these processes generate solid, liquid, and airborne toxic waste, much of which remains in Sarnia. A company with the anodyne name Clean Harbors Environmental Services currently incinerates and landfills hazardous waste on site. In 1958, Imperial Oil began using Sarnia's salt caverns to store their chemical-laden "brine" (also known as "produced water," this is the fluid left over after the oil has been extracted).[93] Later, manufacturers began injecting other industrial wastes into the caverns. However, the waste has a proclivity to seep back up to the surface. In 2012, for example, Sarnia's Centennial Park was forced to close when park users noticed "black, tar-like substance of unknown origin"on the ground.[94] Environmental tests documented unsafe levels of lead, asbestos, and hydrocarbons in the park's soil and grass, which necessitated the demolition of some of the park's infrastructure.

91. "Aamjiwnaang First Nation".
92. Hoover et al., "Indigenous Peoples", 1645.
93. Kent et al., "Subsurface", 380–97.
94. Direct quote from the environmental assessment.

Another site where the toxic byproducts of the petrochemical economy are sequestered is in the bodies of the Aamjiwnaang residents. Biomonitoring studies conducted in 2006 by Environmental Defense Canada found in the blood and urine of one Aamjiwnaang resident sixty-one of the sixty-eight toxic chemicals of concern. Her body burden was the highest measured anywhere in Canada.

The true toll that this is taking on the health of the Aamjiwnaang nation is impossible to tally. The government demurs that the necessary studies would be expensive and time-consuming, and that the tools of science are blunt. It is nearly impossible to prove that any given illness is caused by a given exposure. However, health disparities have been documented:

Women in Chemical Valley were 3.11 times more likely to be hospitalized than other Ontario residents. Men were 2.83 times more likely to require hospitalization. Cardiovascular and respiratory complaints, which are thought to be pollution related, accounted for many hospital admissions.[95]

Around 40 percent of Aamjiwnaang residents use an inhaler. The prevalence of asthma is 17 percent among adults and 22 percent among children.[96] (In the rest of Canada, the rate is 8.5 percent for adults[97] and 13 percent for children[98]).

The ratio of male births declined over the period from 1984 to 1992, from less than 0.5 to about 0.3.[99]

Thirty-nine percent of Aamjiwnaang women experience miscarriages or stillbirths, compared to the Canadian average of 25 percent.

Twenty-three percent of Aamjiwnaang children have learning disabilities compared to four percent of the general Canadian population.[100]

95. Fung et al., "Impact", 18.
96. MacDonald and Rang, "Exposing".
97. Garner and Kohen, "Changes", 45–50.
98. Millar and Gerry, "Childhood", 12.
99. Mackenzie et al., "Declining", 1295–98.
100. "Aamjiwnaang First Nation".

The surface water in Sarnia is so contaminated that residents are warned not to even touch it, let alone drink it, fish, or swim in it. The salt caverns leach industrial waste and brine into the groundwater, which seeps into many of the wells that had been used for drinking water. The salt caverns are leaking; it's hard to predict just when and how much and in what direction the plume will flow. Just like the gooey tar balls that surfaced suddenly at the park, a drinking well might test potable one day and then be ruined the next.

Case Study: Developmental Origins of Health and Disease (DOHAD)

Consumer advocacy groups have lobbied strenuously for limits on certain plastics (particularly those containing BPA and phthalates) in products designed for babies. While infancy and early childhood *are* vulnerable periods, intervening after birth may already be too late. As the thalidomide tragedy demonstrated, it is very challenging to design tests to assure the safety of chemical exposures in pregnant women. Some children born to mothers who had taken thalidomide as prescribed for morning sickness were perfectly healthy. Others were born without arms, or without legs. The difference? It was not the dose that mattered in this case. It was the timing. All of the problems occurred when the drug was used between twenty-one and thirty-six days post-conception. This two-week period is known as a *critical window*. The problem is that we only recognize critical windows in hindsight.

There is an idea that the health of an adult is determined not merely by the choices that they make in adulthood (to smoke or not, to exercise or not, to drink or not), but by what transpired while they were in the womb. This theory is called DOHaD: Developmental Origins of Health and Disease. Again, the lesson was learned from tragedy. Women who had taken a form of synthetic estrogen called diethylstilbestrol (DES) during pregnancy did not immediately show any clinical evidence of harm, nor did their babies. However, when their daughters attained puberty, many of them developed a rare form of cancer: vaginal clear cell adinocarcinoma.[101] Further investigation revealed that the problems were not limited to the daughters. Sons had unusual health risks as well, which were not apparent until they reached early adulthood.[102]

These sorts of delayed adverse responses are not limited to DES; however, data are incomplete. Retrospective studies that aim to characterize exposures during pregnancy are rife with recall bias and other challenges. The National Children's Study was designed to collect biological evidence from pregnant women (such as blood and urine samples) and then to correlate in utero exposures with health outcomes for their offspring in adulthood. Unfortunately, funding for this project was not sustained.[103]

Evidence suggests that some monomers and additives used in plastics, particularly BPA, are developmental toxicants. We do not know exactly when the critical windows are, but early first trimester is a sensitive time for the developing central nervous system, for male and female reproductive systems, the endocrine system, and the immune system, among other endpoints.[104] Some work has been done on characterizing the effects of BPA exposure in the second trimester, but to date, no studies have been undertaken during the third trimester.[105] Another challenge is that toxicology studies are designed to answer questions about one specific endpoint or one body system at a time. In the case of BPA, with effects as varied as weakened tooth enamel[106] and increased susceptibility to addictions as an adult,[107] it is not possible to predict what might be in store for children exposed in utero.

How does this translate into policy? Because harm to future generations may begin with preconception exposures via epigenetic alterations transmitted through either the mother's egg or the

101. Reed and Fenton, "Exposure", 134–46.
102. "DES Sons".
103. "National Children's Study".
104. "Critical Windows".
105. Ibid.
106. European Society of Endocrinology, "Exposure".
107. Suzuki et al., "Prenatal".

father's sperm,[108] *all* people who might someday procreate must be protected.

Thus far, we have been examining how the use of plastics has a direct impact on human health in consumers. The health impacts are more pronounced in resin synthesis and plastic fabrication workers, who tend to be exposed to high doses over long periods of time, and in those who handle plastics that have been discarded.

In the early days of its production, doctors noticed that workers who were handling vinyl chloride[109] were developing acroosteolysis (a condition in which the bones of the fingers begin to dissolve), as well as an otherwise extremely rare form of liver cancer called angiosarcoma. Following allegations (that were later substantiated) that the industry not only knew of the risks, but colluded to keep the data secret, even from government regulators, occupational safety standards were instituted. When these were found to be insufficiently protective, they were lowered. Later, they were lowered again.

Today, the US Environmental Protection Agency describes vinyl chloride as a "Group A" human carcinogen,[110] meaning a substance known to cause cancer in humans.

Burning e-waste to reclaim marketable metals, for example, exposes workers to the toxic fumes of burning plastics. As the next section will explore, however, even plastics that are not burned may have widespread environmental consequences after disposal that lead to another form of indirect harm to human health.

## ABOARD THE *ALGITA*

The most memorable part of my doctoral work was a summer interning with the Algalita Marine Research Foundation in Long Beach, California. I was lucky enough to be invited to sail with

108. Grandjean et al., "Life-long", 10–16.
109. Vinyl chloride is the building block of PVC, which is also called vinyl.
110. "Vinyl chloride".

Captain Charles Moore and his crew on a research trip from Long Beach to the tip of Baja California.

We dropped anchor off the Coronado Islands and then hopped overboard. I turned to find myself face to face with a sea lion. I held my breath for a moment and stayed very still. It turned a somersault. So did I. We played while fish I cannot begin to describe flitted around us. And not a single plastic bag floated by.

Surfacing, I saw in the distance cliffs that looked chalky white. I wondered aloud if they were like the white cliffs of Dover. "Nope," Charlie told me. "They're just covered in bird shit."

What I didn't realize at the time was that these bird droppings themselves were part of my sea-plastic tour. The food chain, of course, is made up not only of what goes in, but also of what comes out. Nutrients consumed but then not needed are released back into the ecosystem. The polite term for this process is "egestion." Perhaps more important to our story is *where* the nutrients are re-introduced into circulation. Whales dive deep to hunt for squid, then return to the surface to breathe. Around them swirl copious plumes of poo. These nutrients transported up from the depths feed neustonic organisms like phytoplankton and algae. These in turn are the sustenance for the krill and zooplankton, around which fish flourish. The sea birds I saw on the cliffs feast on this abundance, and then circle back to land with their bellies full, some of which they regurgitate to their chicks. The rest they digest themselves. Their nutrient-rich droppings bring the deep sea's life-giving minerals, including phosphorus, to land. Unfortunately, it turns out that the biological pump, as this cycle is known, is becoming increasingly clogged with plastic.[111]

It begins with the zooplankton. Zooplankton glean the tiniest fragments (less than one millimeter) of plastic marine debris. Because the plastic is not readily broken down in their bodies, it (or at least *some* of it . . . whether any is retained in their digestive tract is a question that to my knowledge has not been answered) finds its way out into their fecal pellets. When zooplankton in an experimental setting were fed Styrofoam, one unfortunate consequence

111. Intagliata, "Whale Poop"; Provencher et al., "Garbage", 1477–84.

of this unsavory addition was that the pellets tended to be less dense.[112] As they drifted on the currents in the water column, that voluminous space between the sun-lit surface waters and the benthos, they remained a temptation to hungry fish for twice as long as is typical for usually faster-sinking poo. When these fecal pellets are eaten, rather than sinking to the seafloor, the poisons that they contain continue moving through the food web.

That food harvested from the sea is full of plastic should no longer surprise any reader. In study after study, when samples of fish and shellfish sold in markets around the world are analyzed, plastic is found.[113] Van Cauwenberghe and Janssen estimate that adults who eat mollusks, like clams and oysters, may be eating up to eleven thousand microplastic particles per year from shellfish alone, not counting the plastics in the rest of their diet.[114] Knowing that some of these plastic bits came not directly from litter but indirectly, by way of poo, makes the prospect all the more unappealing.

Thinking of how plastics, and plastic-laced prey, and even plastic-laced poo may be entering the food chain at every trophic level, I have begun to wonder if we ought to add a new term to our risk assessment models. Instead of thinking only of how contaminants like mercury increase in concentration as big fish eat smaller fish (a concept called biomagnification), we might consider accounting for what I would call *plastic-mediated magnification*. Perhaps this would help those who continue to complain about unsightly plastic debris as an aesthetic issue to see it for the planetary health crisis that it is.

## SHIFTING DISCOURSE ON MARINE DEBRIS

The problem of plastic marine debris, and more broadly speaking, of society's garbage footprint, was first framed as an aesthetic problem. Articles such as the *Washington Post*'s 2015 piece "Why

112. Cole et al., "Microplastics", 3239–46.

113. Rochman et al. "Anthropogenic", 14340; Romeo et al., "First Evidence", 358–61; Van Cauwenberghe and Janssen, "Microplastics", 65–70.

114. Van Cauwenberghe and Janssen, "Microplastics", 65–70.

Clean Beaches Are So Important if You Want A Relaxing Vacation"
bemoan the unsightly debris that besmirches the otherwise "re-
storative" and "fascinating" seaside summers of the privileged.[115]
This frame tends to perpetuate a cognitive split between places
that are "pristine" and places that are "spoiled." The solution is to
preserve the "pristine" certain places by shifting the contamination
to other places that are already "spoiled." These repositories of refuse are termed "sacrifice zones." The people who live there, or the
workers who move the refuse, are rarely centered in this discourse.

These days, the dominant discourse on plastics frames it as
a conservation biology problem. Much like the split in the aesthetic frame between clean and dirty places, the environmental
frame postulates that while plastics belong in the built environment and are at home in the urban landscape, they should not be
permitted to stray into the wild. People appear in this narrative
either as villains (those who litter, with those who litter on beaches
being especially nefarious) or as saviors (those who recycle and
who volunteer for beach cleanup days). This framing relies on tes-
timony by surfers, snorkelers, and sailors who have encountered
the "plastic soup" first-hand. These stories tend to be illustrated
with gruesome photographs of turtles entangled in six pack rings
that deform them and stunt their growth, or turtles with straws in
their noses, or dolphins drowning in ghost fishing nets, or dead
birds with stomachs full of bottle caps and cigarette lighters. This
discourse centers the suffering of innocent wildlife. If we would
only consume plastic "responsibly" and "manage" our waste as in-
structed, it would not escape into the environment. There is even a
movement afoot to "manage" our wastewater so that plastic fibers
and microbeads can be collected before the water is released. What
is not clear is what will be done with the plastic that we capture.
(More on this later.)

The third frame is that plastics pose a public health problem. The distinction that must be maintained here is between
that which is external to our bodies and that which is internal.
The "environment" is everything outside our bodies. We may look

115. Mooney, "Ocean trash".

the other way when industrial chemicals are found in seawater or in the blubber of whales, but when the contaminants are found in *us*—in our blood or urine, or in our babies' cord blood, this is "toxic trespass." The problem is cast as one that can be addressed by risk assessment. Technicians working in this worldview labor at collecting samples of blood, urine, and baby teeth in order to document and contrast the body burdens in varying populations. Toxicologists are busy calculating how much of these contaminants we can absorb before disease processes are triggered. Microscopic bits of Styrofoam circulating in our bloodstream should be no cause for alarm as long as there are not *too many* of them. The baseline for what constitutes a "normal" proportion of synthetic material in the human body (which, in reality, is zero) is ever shifting.

## ABUNDANCE

The abundance of plastics in the ocean, and our knowledge of it, is growing so quickly that whatever I write here will be outdated long before you hold this book in your hands. Nevertheless, I would be remiss not to include a few of the most often-quoted numbers. According to the United Nations Environment Program, there are forty-six thousand pieces of plastic litter per square mile (thirteen thousand pieces in every square kilometer) of ocean surface, which is not confined to the gyres.[116] To the estimated fifty-one trillion pieces of microplastics in the world's oceans, each year we add eight million metric tons more.[117] In a 2011 study, samples from the Antarctic Ocean had up to 42,826 pieces of plastic per square kilometer. And all of this is just skimming the surface.

The US EPA estimates that 54 percent of manufactured plastic sinks. Even the plastics that are buoyant sink once colonized by fouling organisms. As Five Gyres co-founder Marcus Eriksen conjectures: "It is likely that sedimentation is the ultimate

116. Gjerde, *Ecosystems.*
117. "'Turn the tide'".

fate for plastic lost at sea".[118] In an interview with *Orion*, Richard Thompson, a marine biologist at the University of Plymouth, UK, estimated that 20 percent of what appeared to be sand on the beach in Plymouth, England is actually not fragmented rock but instead fragmented plastic. He immediately qualified that he believes the figure of 20 percent to be an underestimate.[119] Later research proved them correct: *All* of the crustaceans that Alan Jamieson and his team collected from the bottom of the Mariana Trench—10,890 meters deep—had eaten plastic.[120]

In addition to the microplastics floating unquantified through the water column and littering the largely unexplored sea floor, nanoplastics, too, escape standard trawls.[121]

No one knows how much plastic is already hidden in the bodies of sea dwellers. Perhaps the comparison that plastic fragments will soon outnumber fish is understating the problem. Soon we may not be able to speak of "fish" as something distinct from "plastic." Or, for that matter, of ourselves: human beings have the strange distinction of being both the source of plastic and its sink.

Initially we tried to demarcate the plastics that humans released from the decks of ships from that we spilled from shore—the 639,000 plastic cargo containers that fall into the sea each *day*[122] from the land-based discharges that are at least four times that amount.[123] We tried to count butts and bags and bottles to apportion blame more accurately. In the last ten years, plastic drink bottle litter has increased by 67 percent, plastic bags by 54 percent, and cigarette butts by 44 percent.[124] But the bottles and bags and butts are not to blame, nor are the people who used them last. The problem is not that they were thrown away; it is that they were made at all.

118. Eriksen et al., "Nature".
119. Weisman, "Polymers".
120. "Man-Made Fibres".
121. Galloway, "Micro-and Nano-plastics".
122. Derriak, "Pollution", 842–52.
123. UNEP, "Marine Litter".
124. Snowden and Fanshawe, "Beachwatch".

We have no plan for managing plastic waste properly. Short of financially viable, closed-loop recycling, we have no recourse but to burn it (either in incinerators or as reclaimed fuel) or to contain it in the hope that future generations will have a better idea. Marine plastics are a reminder that our efforts to contain it are doomed to failure. Think of how difficult it would be to gather confetti from along a stretch of beach. Now imagine that the area you are trying to clean is not only miles long but also miles deep. Remember that some of it floats, some of it has sunk to the sea floor, and some swirls below the surface. More is constantly being added. While some of the plastic debris is large enough to be scooped out, much of it consists of tiny plastic fragments. If we were to sieve out pieces that small, we would inevitably capture tiny fish and plankton as well. The by-catch would be impossible to sort without harming the marine life. Charles Moore likens the task to trying to empty a bathtub with a thimble while the faucet is still running [3].[125]

Meanwhile, the "Plastisphere"[126] is taking on a life of its own. Floating plastic is not only colonized by benign fouling organisms like barnacles and seaweed. Invasive and sometimes pathogenic organisms find their reach expanded beyond their previous limits. In what researchers call "the longest documented transoceanic survival and dispersal of coastal species by rafting",[127] 289 species including *Vibrio* bacteria (the pathogen responsible for cholera) floated to the U.S. Pacific Northwest on debris from the Japanese tsunami.[128]. When fecal pathogens like *Vibrio* find their way onto plastic "rafts," it seems they survive for longer periods of time than they otherwise would, potentially endangering, among others, swimmers at recreational beaches.[129]

125. "Mid-Ocean Plastics".

126. A term coined in 2013 by Erik R. Zettler, Tracy J. Mincer, and Linda A. Amaral-Zettler (Zettler et al., "Life").

127. Carlton et al., "Tsunami-driven", 1402–06.

128. Kirstein et al., "Dangerous", 1–8; Oberbeckmann et al., "Marine", 551–62.

129. Quilliam et al., "Seaweeds", 201–07.

Of course, plastic debris poses not only a biological threat but also a chemical one. We know someone by the company they keep. Plastic debris attracts persistent organic chemicals to itself, concentrating them at up to one million times the levels in ambient seawater, and accelerating their biomagnification in the marine food web.[130] The greater the surface area of the plastic, the higher the concentration of adsorbed contaminants is likely to be.

Numerous studies have shown that ingested plastic particles are deleterious to the health of marine life.[131] Nanoparticles of polystyrene dramatically impair the reproduction of freshwater zooplankton and green algae.[132] Larger polystyrene particles also impair the survival of marine copepod *Calanus helgolandicus*.[133] Marine worms' energy reserves dwindle when exposed to tiny particles of polyvinyl chloride.[134] Adaptive behavior may be affected, leaving prey more vulnerable to predation, as Culum Brown and his colleagues demonstrated in beachhoppers exposed to microplastics.[135]

The obvious physical properties of plastics explain much of the harm. Ingested plastic may obstruct the digestive tract, preventing food from passing through. In an example of tragic irony, this token of a culture predicated on the unquenchable thirst for endless growth may impart in its victims a sense of satiety, discouraging them from seeking out nutritive sustenance.

But as Chelsea Rochman and others have shown, ingested microplastics can also transfer toxic chemicals into fish and birds.[136] We are now waiting for science to tell us whether we have some special superpower that protects us from the same fate.

These chemicals are both those that are intentionally used to manufacture plastics as well as those compounds that a plastic

130. Mato et al., "Plastic Resin", 318–24; Teuten et al., "Potential", 7759–64.

131. Rochman et al., "Ecological", 302–12.

132. Besseling et al., "Nanoplastic", 12336–43.

133. Cole et al. "Impact", 1130–37.

134. Wright et al., "Microplastic Ingestion", R1031–33.

135. Tosetto et al., "Microplastics", 199.

136. Rochman et al., "Anthropogenic", 14340; Rochman et al., "Ingested".

draws to itself from the seawater. Most of the research discusses persistent organic pollutants (POPs)—a notoriously unhealthy class of chemicals that are attracted to fat and therefore build up over time in the food web and in our bodies. It is this very affinity for fats and oils that explains why they stick to plastic marine debris: what loves fat almost always hates water. When these chemicals are in seawater, they will attach themselves to just about anything to get out, including sediment. Plastics share this attribute, called lipophilicity-hydrophobicity. This is why it made sense to focus on POPs.

But there are many other ways that plastics attract environmental chemicals, and for this reason polymers are used as environmental sampling media, as well as for water filtration. Metals are another class with an affinity for plastic. Karen Ashton found that polyethylene pellets suspended in seawater for eight weeks adsorbed lead and cadmium.[137] Nakashima et al. quantified chromium (Cr), cadmium (Cd), tin (Sn), antimony (Sb), and lead (Pb) in plastic litter collected during beach surveys in Japan.[138] Holmes et al. also quantified trace metals (Cr, Co, Ni, Cu, Zn, Cd and Pb) in polyethylene pellets.[139]

But no one was looking for the most famous heavy metal that we think of when we discuss seafood contamination, although several specialty polymers have been designed to attract mercury.[140] It isn't hard to do. Mercury has a particular affinity for sulfur

137. Ashton et al., "Association", 2050–55.

138. Nakashima et al., "Quantification", 10099–105.

139. Holmes et al. , "Adsorption", 42–48.

140. A team from the University of Genova found that Duolite GT-73, a poly-styrene/divinylbenzene resin, adsorbed significant amounts of mercury chloride over a twenty-four-hour period when immersed in a neutral to basic solution (Chiarle et al., "Mercury", 2971–78). In 2004, Pohl and Prusisz used Duolite to preconcentrate Hg(II) from hydrochloric acid media. (Dow's Duolight is now marketed under the name Amberlite GT73 for Rohn & Haas [see "Amberlite"].) Another study compared the performance of organic resins Purolite S-920 from Bro-Tech Corporation, Ionac SR-4 from Sybron Chemicals, and SIR-200 from Resin Tech in their ability to adsorb mercury from industrial effluent (Fondeur et al., "Mercury"). Each of these is also polystyrene crosslinked with divinyl benzene, with thiol functional groups bonded to the

molecules, and a previous experiment using a polymer containing sulfur and limonene drew mercury out of drinking water.[141] I wondered whether some types of conventional plastic marine debris that contain sulfur could also adsorb mercury, so I designed an experiment to find out.

Two common commercial resins, styrene-butadiene and polychloroprene, incorporate thiolate (sulfur-hydrogen) molecules. Thiolates are also known as "mercaptans", which is derived from the Latin *mercurium captans* ("that which captures mercury"). Mercaptan salts are used as chain transfer agents in the emulsion (but not ionic solution) polymerizations of synthetic rubber in order to control the molecular weight of the finished product (although dibenzyltrithiocarbonate, which is not a mercaptan, is sometimes substituted).[142]

As I do not have sufficient training to handle mercury safely,[143] I contracted with Brooks Rand lab (now Brooks Applied Labs) to conduct the experiment. Technicians shredded preconsumer styrene-butadiene and polychloroprene and immersed it in vials of Puget Sound seawater that had been spiked with an environmentally relevant concentration (one hundred nanograms per liter) of methyl mercury. Using EPA Method 1631, the total mercury was measured after seventy-two hours. The styrene-butadiene pieces had adsorbed 72 percent of the mercury from the seawater, and the polychloroprene (in separate vials) 17 percent. This finding supported my hypothesis, but the sample size (three control and three experimental replicates for each substrate) was too small to count.

---

polystyrene. Heavy metal ions were captured on active filters composed by a conducting surface covered by poly-4-vinylpyridine or polyacrylic acid Due to respective pyridine and carboxylate groups those polymer films have chelating properties for heavy metals (Pascal et al., "New Concept", 3263–69).

141. Carter, "Researchers".

142. Senyek et al., "Dibenzyltrithiocarbonate".

143. Even those with significant experience have accidents, as the tragic death of Karen Wetterhahn, a senior researcher on toxic metals at Dartmouth College, illustrates.

Funding from NOAA Sea Grant allowed me to repeat the tests, this time adding more variety. Technicians tested seven replicates each of polycarbonate resin pellets (Acros Organics #178310050, lot A0287290), styrene/butadiene ABA block copolymer (30 percent styrene) crumbs (Scientific Polymer Products #057, lot 600503005), and post-consumer recycled rubber crumbs intended for use as a surface covering for playgrounds (Playsafer Rubber Products). The styrene/butadiene ABA block copolymer again outperformed the others, this time adsorbing 58 percent of the mercury compared to the rubber crumbs' 15 percent. This time, however, we had a surprise. Polycarbonate, rather than adsorbing mercury, *released* it. After introducing the polycarbonate into the test tube, the level of mercury in the seawater rose by 8.6 nanograms per liter. The mercury may have been an intentional additive, perhaps as an antimicrobial or as an optical clarifier, but all of this is merely speculation. What industry puts in plastics, and why, remains a trade secret. This is also why the composition of commodity plastics varies from batch to batch, making it quite difficult to replicate experiments using them.

One of the missing pieces of this line of research is that I don't know what happens when a fish eats plastic that has concentrated mercury. Does the mercury stay in the plastic and pass through the fish, or does the acidic environment of the digestive tract leach the mercury back out again? Over time, does eating plastic laced with mercury increase the level of mercury in the flesh of the fish? I considered doing further experiments to find out, but that would involve intentionally exposing fish to a known poison, and in the end, killing them—treating them as merely instrumentally valuable rather than as creatures with inherent worth and dignity. If I were to do this, I would be reproducing disposable culture.

# 3

## The Spiritual Impact of Plastics

IN ONE OF MY favorite stories, Balaam's faithful donkey saves his life. Balaam, who is on his way to deliver bad news to the king of Moab, is understandably preoccupied with his precarious political fortunes. He does not see the angry angel with a drawn sword blocking his path. The donkey sees, though, and three times brings Balaam out of harm's way. Balaam beats the donkey and scolds her for disobedience, but the donkey finds her voice and talks back.[1]

Not only could the donkey see the angel of the Lord where the human could not, but even after all their years together, Balaam could not truly see his own donkey. She was instrumental to him—simply a means of conveyance. Because of this, she was also fungible—interchangeable with any other donkey. When she did not follow his lead, he reminded her that she was replaceable: "I wish I had a sword in my hand! I would kill you right now!" In reply, the donkey reminds him of their relationship: "Am I not your donkey, which you have ridden all your life to this day? Have I been in the habit of treating you this way?" Balaam concedes the point, and in so doing, acknowledges her as an individual. Only then is he able to see the angel.

Consumerism depends on our collective agreement to pretend that the world is instrumental and fungible. When products—or relationships—no longer meet our needs, we discard them and replace them. Planned obsolescence ensures that nothing will be left to pass on to future generations. Conditioned by the fear that these insidious messages arouse, we begin to see ourselves and each other in the same ways, and to compete not only for resources, but for attention. Judging, and a fear of being judged,

---

1. Bamidbar/Numbers 22:21–34

dominate where mutuality and a relational ethic of care could be. This is what I mean by disposable culture.

Our relationship with the natural world suffers in disposable culture. Complexity is reduced to one-dimensionality. A forest becomes nothing more than a site of lucrative industry, or a purveyor of ecosystem services that must be managed. A mountain landscape conceals coal deposits, and, following the logic of disposable culture, must therefore be removed. Cattle and chickens are for food, nothing more, and following the logic of disposable culture, are most efficiently raised in confined animal feedlots. We steel ourselves against sentimentality. We foreclose any possibility of a relationship with these places and their inhabitants.

This mentality cannot be compartmentalized easily. The disposable spirit measures its own worth, and that of others, based on their productivity, or on their accumulated wealth. Everything and everyone is disposable, fungible, and instrumental.

In contrast, there is no waste in nature. Nutrients and energy cycle endlessly from trophic level to trophic level. It is an economy of abundance. Nothing is ever diminished by use. Nothing is lost; it merely changes hands (or paws, or branches), and even that impermanently. We cannot hold our breath more than a few minutes, at most. The life-giving oxygen and carbon dioxide circulating within our bodies must be released back into general circulation so as to be available to others. Sometimes elements appear stuck, like the mercury and carbon sequestered in the frozen vegetation buried under permafrost,[2] but looking in deep time, we see that they are still circulating as easily as is our breath. The gift economy of nature is not unlike the human gift economy that Lewis Hyde describes: "Whatever we have been given is supposed to be given away again, not kept . . . the essential is this, that the gift must move."[3]

Though historical records are equivocal, thinking of the land and its bounty as something borrowed and lasting rather than as a possession that could be used up may have restrained the human

2. Schuster et al., "Permafrost", 1463–71.

3. Hyde, *Gift*.

tendency to pollute in ancient Hebrew society. Ched Myers writes, "At its root, Sabbath observance is about gifts and limits: the grace of receiving that which the Creator gives, and the responsibility not to take too much, nor to mistake the gift for a possession."[4] It rests on the principle that land cannot be sold in perpetuity, for God remains the true owner of the land. Every fiftieth year is a jubilee, when certain land titles revert back to their original owners and slaves are freed. The Leviticus text also prescribes that between jubilees, every seventh year the land must rest. All human agricultural activity must pause so that nature can regenerate, mirroring the solemn commandment for all people and animals to rest one day every week. Today, the word *waste* is sometimes used to describe land that is uncultivated, rhetorically transforming this virtue into a sin.

Not all wasting is alike.

In Betty Smith's 1943 novel *A Tree Grows in Brooklyn*, the young protagonist, Francie, looks forward to pouring her mug of coffee down the drain each day. "It was one of the links between the ground-down poor and the wasteful rich . . . even if she had less than anybody in Williamsburg, somehow she was more. She was richer because she had something to waste."[5]

People living with poverty are often blamed for wasting: wasting time, wasting opportunities, wasting money that could be put towards rent on some small indulgence that might make life bearable. Those who create and sustain wealth inequality hope that by shaming them, they can deflect attention from themselves. We are supposed to believe that 80 percent of the world's population lives on less than ten dollars a day[6] due to their own moral failings. Not to mention that of these, over three billion are living on less than two dollars and fifty cents a day. Most faith traditions align with John the Baptist's teaching: "If you have two coats, share with someone who has none. And if you have food, do likewise."[7] Yet

4. Myers, *Biblical.*
5. Smith, *Tree.*
6. Shah, "Poverty".
7. Luke 3:11.

today we are trained to admire instead the intelligence and cunning of those who hoard and those who exploit.

Rather than focusing on Francie's spilled coffee, then, I decry the waste of human life that inevitably follows from disposable culture. I decry the twenty-two thousand children under five who die each *day* of poverty-related causes.[8] I decry the waste of non-human lives. According to the International Union for Conservation of Nature, we are losing species at a rate ten thousand times higher than the background rate that has prevailed for millennia.[9] None of us wants this.

Some would reassure us that nature has been here long before us and will outlast us. The power of nature to regenerate and adapt seems boundless. We think that all of the natural world is as resilient as the tardigrade—that virtually indestructible microscopic creature that has been found to adapt to temperatures from −459°F (absolute zero) to 304°F (recall that water boils at 212°F). Tardigrades have survived starvation, desiccation, ionizing radiation, and even the vacuum of outer space. However, they do this by entering an altered state called cryptobiosis, in which their metabolic rate slows until it is almost imperceptible. The usually plump moss piglet, as the tardigrade is sometimes called, sheds its skin, retracts its legs, and becomes an unrecognizable dimpled blob incapable of self-directed movement.

So the earth responds when humans abuse it. Certainly, it will outlast us, but in what form? For decades some policy makers have acted as if "the solution to pollution is dilution."[10] As a result, too much carbon dioxide now overwhelms the atmosphere and the oceans. Too much nitrogen runoff (much of it from fertilizer) seeps into rivers and bays, leading to dead zones. Too many novel toxicants, like the long-chain perfluorinated compounds, renowned commercially for their stability and persistence, have entered the environment where they are impairing the immune systems and endocrine systems of countless species, including hu-

8. "Child mortality".
9. Hood, "Biodiversity".
10. Attributed to Sherry A. Rogers, MD.

mans. Too many fragments of disposable plastic are dispersed into the soil and the sea, carrying these toxicants into the food chain.

Nature is trying to reabsorb the anthropogenic wastes of the Plasticene. The fungus *Rhodotorula taiwanensis* strain MD1149 can remediate radioactive waste.[11] Mealworms (*Tenebrio molitor* larvae) are learning to digest polystyrene.[12] *Ideonella sakaiensis* 201-F6 bacteria have evolved to produce an enzyeme (PETase) that breaks down polyethylene terephthalate, the plastic from which most single-use water bottles are made.[13] The fungi *Pestalotiopsis microspora* and *Aspergillus tubingensis*[14] attack polyurethane,[15] and various microbes are learning to eat polyvinyl chloride[16] and polystyrene[17].

However, we are producing toxic substrates much more quickly than evolution can assimilate them. And consider that we produce three hundred million tons of new plastic a year.[18] If we were to raise a commensurate mass of microbes, we would have a different, but no less serious, problem on our hands. Many microorganisms, including fungi, are potentially pathogenic to crops, wildlife, and humans, and just as they can evolve to subsist on novel sources of nutrition, they can evolve resistance to drugs and to environmental conditions that ordinarily would keep them in check.

Nor is this a technological problem that can be solved by simply switching to throwaway goods made of, and packaged with, biodegradable materials. If we continue to cultivate a habit of treating things as disposable, people will continue to see themselves and each other as disposable, too. We will think nothing of converting a field of corn into throwaway plastic packaging while

---

11. Tkavc et al., "Prospects", 2528.

12. Charlotte Frank, personal communication.

13. Yoshida et al., "Bacterium", 1196–99.

14. Khan et al., "Biodegradation", 469–80.

15. Russell et al., "Biodegradation".

16. Kumar et al., "Screening".

17. Shah et al., "Biological Degradation", 246–65.

18. Wassener, "Raising Awareness".

others go hungry. Like the tardigrade entering cryptobiosis, the human spirit suffocating in disposable culture shrivels and becomes unrecognizable.

## Disposable Culture Unwrapped

Plastic marine debris was not considered an urgent issue until a wealthy white yachtsman called attention to the plastic trash he saw in the North Pacific gyre on his way home from the Los Angeles to Honolulu Trans-Pac Yacht Race. Later, photos of albatrosses on the Midway Atoll, their bellies fatally filled with plastics, commanded widespread public sympathy. Scientists documented plastic fragments and fibers, along with their invisible toxic constituents, in fish being sold for human consumption. Now, the European Union has declared a "War on Plastic," vowing to make all plastic reusable or recyclable by 2030.[19] The United Nations, too, has prioritized the problem. Prime Minister Justin Trudeau announced that Canada would use their presidency in the G7 as a platform for advocating for plastic marine debris reduction.[20]

In Mathare Valley (Nairobi, Kenya), back in 1993, I saw open drainage ditches full of human excrement and plastic trash forming the boundaries of the dirt paths that wound between the densely packed homes. They had already been there for a very long time. Children scavenged in landfills for resalable scrap metals as well as for anything still edible. That millions of people around the world live in, work in, and hunt for food in mounds of garbage does not seem to stir public imagination as much as the sight of a turtle with a straw stuck in its nose.[21]

One explanation for this compassion gap is that residents of Mathare Valley, and others living with extreme poverty, are somehow assumed to be complicit in their own suffering. Because charismatic marine fauna are indisputably blameless, however,

19. Boffey, "EU Declares".
20. Nowlan, "International Plastics".
21. "Sea Turtle".

they point the finger of accusation back at us. And that provokes enough discomfort to spur us to action.

In the gaze of some, Mathare Valley confirms the classist narrative of meritocracy: If the residents took better care of their neighborhood and picked up their trash, they too could have safer and more hygienic surroundings. They "reason" that this proves that providing "nice things" to "those people" would be a *waste*, because they wouldn't take care of it anyway. And thus excused from culpability, they resume their own daily activities, willfully ignorant that some of the trash they see in photos of Agbogbloshie, Ghana[22] or Wen'an, China[23] may have come from their own blue bins. When confronted with this, they point out that more of the trash in these infamous wastelands originated locally. Therefore, generating trash, and sending it "away" for more socio-economically vulnerable people to deal with, is rendered morally acceptable. This perspective fits neatly with the "waste management" ideology that the problem is not plastics, or other bits of trash themselves, but irresponsible people. This false morality is supported by a religious orientation toward individual purity, which I will discuss below.

It is not an either/or situation. Both the plight of the turtle impaled on a plastic straw and the suffering of humans have the same root cause: disposable culture. Just as "the cry of the earth and the cry of the poor are one,"[24] so our Biblical call to enact compassion towards the most marginalized among us and the call to respect creation are one and the same.

## TOWARDS AN ECO-THEOLOGY OF ZERO WASTE

I approach this section with caution, as I am by no means a theologian. I am simply a person of faith tracing the influence of the

22. Minter, "Burning Truth".
23. Minter, "Plastic".
24. Attributed to Pope Francis.

Christian[25] sacred stories that have shaped my thinking about waste.

Ecologists today often speak of "keystone species" that perform essential "ecosystem services." They argue, following Robert Paine, that our conservation efforts should focus on these species; the others are "redundant."[26] Paul's letter to the church in Corinth uses the metaphor of a body with many parts to describe a very different ecology, one in which no one is expendable or redundant:

> Indeed, the body does not consist of one member but of many. If the foot would say, "Because I am not a hand, I do not belong to the body," that would not make it any less a part of the body . . . If all were a single member, where would the body be? As it is, there are many members, yet one body. The eye cannot say to the hand, "I have no need of you," nor again the head to the feet, "I have no need of you." *On the contrary, the members of the body that seem to be weaker are indispensable.*[27]

This reversal, in which the weaker members merit more consideration than do the stronger, is fully congruent with the recurring Biblical theme that God will reclaim (and, indeed, honor) what has been rejected:

> Jesus said to them, "Have you never read in the scriptures: 'The stone that the builders rejected has become the cornerstone; this was the Lord's doing, and it is amazing in our eyes'?"[28]

This goes far beyond a call to reduce, reuse, and recycle. It seems that the piles of trash, and the people who live among them, are more precious in God's accounting than are the wealthy consumers who produced both situations: *"He picks up the poor from out of the dirt, rescues the wretched who've been thrown out with the trash,*

25. I would like to acknowledge here that much of what is referred to as "Christian" is actually appropriated from other traditions, particularly from Judaism as well as from various earth-centered religions.

26. Paine, "Food Web", 65–75.

27. 1 Cor 12:12–26 (emphasis mine).

28. Matt. 21:42 and Ps. 118:22–23.

*Seats them among the honored guests, a place of honor among the brightest and best."*[29]

A parable attributed to Jesus of Nazareth condones the seemingly irrational behavior of a hypothetical shepherd who leaves ninety-nine sheep unguarded to go off in search of one who is missing:

> *"What do you think? If a shepherd has a hundred sheep, and one of them has gone astray, does he not leave the ninety-nine on the mountains and go in search of the one that went astray? And if he finds it, truly I tell you, he rejoices over it more than over the ninety-nine that never went astray. So it is not the will of your Father in heaven that one of these little ones should be lost."*[30]

Sheep are intelligent and sociable. They remember absent members of their flock and recognize them upon their return, even when years have passed. Likewise, they remember human faces. Sheep stay together, unless the arrival of a predator scatters the flock. When a sheep finds itself separated from the fold, it experiences "severe stress and panic." One farmer described to me how an isolated sheep will lie on the ground, bleating, paralyzed in terror. In other words, it becomes easy prey.

When I read this parable with children in Godly Play classes, we ask ourselves, "Who am I in this story?" I find it easiest to imagine myself as the isolated sheep, letting a powerful sense of relief wash over me as I recognize my shepherd approaching. I can put myself in the place of the other sheep, anxiously awaiting the return of our separated friend. As the story is framed, though, the listener is clearly in the role of a shepherd, who is not only responsible for the collective flock, but also for the well being of each particular sheep. They recognize each other. They see each other. In God's design, each one matters. None is disposable or fungible.

In contrast, consider this excerpt from a recent article on pollinators in almond fields. Here the bees are entirely instrumental and the beekeeper views the hives as functional units rather than

29. Tehillim/Ps. 113:7–8 (The Message)
30. Matt. 18:12–14, Luke 15:3–7.

through a relational lens: "Any loss of a BOB (blue orchard bee) female matters: it permanently reduces the current year's pollination workforce and diminishes next year's crew because fewer eggs are laid. The loss of one honeybee, in contrast, is trivial because a healthy colony generates tens of thousands of workers across a year."[31]

Again, attributed to Jesus of Nazareth are specific instructions not to let any food go to waste. *"When they were filled, He said to His disciples, "Gather up the leftover fragments so that nothing will be lost. So they gathered them up, and from the fragments of the five barley loaves, left by those who had eaten, they filled twelve baskets."*[32] He is reported to have said this *after* the miraculous feeding of the crowds. The motivation, then, is not a problem of scarcity. A child's gift of five loaves and two fishes had just sated over five thousand people. The gathering of twelve baskets of leftovers demonstrates that there is more than enough food. I wonder if this is retold as a reminder that God counts each crumb, and if it serves instead to reinforce the same message as Jesus's choice of associates: God gathers those seen as inconsequential by society.

These five thousand people had gathered, presumably because for most of them hope was otherwise hard to come by. They were all under the rule of the Roman Empire, which did not countenance dissent. Watching the twelve baskets fill with crumbs, did some of them remember God's promise that the descendants of the twelve tribes of Israel would one day be too numerous to count? Were they reminded that collectively they might have more power than Rome thought possible?

I searched my faith tradition in vain for any counterexamples, but was unable to find a single injunction *to* waste.[33] There is

31. Embry, "Building".

32. John 6:12–13.

33. I do not have space in this essay to consider the instances in which soldiers were ordered to *lay waste* to besieged cities and not leave anyone alive. The critical question of whether war is ever morally justifiable I will leave for another day.

nowhere I am enjoined to treat anyone or anything as disposable, as fungible, or as instrumental.

Yet, I am inundated with precisely those messages every day from advertisers. One tempting strategy for coping with the contradiction would be religious ritual, which is often where cognitive dissonance goes to be resolved. (Beware your faith if it answers more questions than it raises!) Ironically, disposable culture itself is now presented as sacrament.

Individually plastic-wrapped sterile packets of wafer and grape juice are become (symbols of) the body and blood of Christ. The fact that no human hands have touched the elements since they were ensconced in plastic is a selling point. I concede that if an immunocompromised individual would otherwise be unable to take communion, this is necessary and good. In most other instances, however, we are just deluding ourselves that God sends grace wrapped in tidy packages. The reality is that Jesus of Nazareth healed with spit and mud.[34] He was a harsh critic of the pious Pharisees and Sadducees, who followed the letter of the law meticulously, but who often fell short in embodying the Spirit.

The idea of sin, and our anxieties related to it, have been seized and twisted by consumerism and by its affiliated (co-opted) religious institutions. In order to divert our attention from real injustices, the approach has been to trivialize our moral responsibilities. Particularly if we are full-bodied, we are shamed for enjoying high-calorie or particularly delicious desserts, which are described as "sinful" or "decadent." On the other hand, we are congratulated as virtuous when we find a good bargain, as if we can somehow claim credit for the low price, even when its production involved the slave labor or child labor or the use of toxic chemicals that harm both workers and the environment. Greed and envy are normalized, as we are conditioned to equate covetousness with healthy ambition.

This strategy also serves to create demand for disposable products. Advertisers would have us think that allowing our body to have a discernible scent—unless it is one we purchase—is

34. Mark 7:31–37 and 8:22–26.

tantamount to sin. We use the same word, "spotless," to describe an innocent spirit that we use to describe a glass rinsed in softened water. Likewise, "dirty" can describe something morally impure or something exposed to soil. And so on. Of course, the only way to possess these sterile and spotless products, which by extension reflect our own aspirations to purity, is by replacing them frequently. Our obsession with individual purity enables disposable culture, and disposable culture continues to separate us from those considered impure.

A man who had been estranged from his biological family was overjoyed to be invited home for Thanksgiving dinner. They had not shared a meal together since his family had found out that he was gay. Learning that he was HIV-positive had brought new urgency to his desire for reconciliation. When he arrived, though, instead of being seated at the table, he was sent outside to eat on the back steps, alone, from a paper plate and with plastic cutlery. When he told me this story, years later, he had tears in his eyes. To be fair, his family probably was not aware (or, at least, not convinced) that HIV cannot be transmitted through casual contact and at least some of their motivation can be attributed to fear. The rest seems to be a symbolic message that the relationship is no longer based in intimacy.

As an alternative, imagine Eucharist being celebrated by sipping wine from a chalice passed from hand to hand, reinscribing that all who drink from a common cup share one common fate. With its emphasis on the re-membering of the body of Christ, we might think of *Communion*, then, as one reminder that God is only made known in *community*.

## SOLUTIONS

This eco-theology calls for a shift from the ethic of instrumental value on which consumerism depends to a recognition of the inherent worth of all of creation. When we treat creation as disposable, we become conditioned to regard ourselves and each other in the same way.

I view this as a corrective to the thread of environmentalist discourse that imposes undue guilt and shame, and that advocates ever-increasing sacrifice. Each of us deserves to have our needs met. We owe no apology for taking up space. We have inherent worth. Rather than self-effacement, let's strive for seeing ourselves and each other fully.

I propose as a remedy a two-pronged approach, involving both our actions and our vision. I have found that these are joined in a positive feedback loop. Starting with either will reinforce the other.

First, whenever possible choose a reusable alternative to disposable products. For example, I carry a lightweight stainless-steel plate and bamboo cutlery set in my backpack. I carry a reusable water bottle and a supply of clean handkerchiefs, so that I do not have to take disposable cups or plates or forks or napkins. I carry cloth shopping bags. Instead of sequestering each vegetable in its own plastic bag, I throw it all in one cloth bag (which I wash every week). At home, I use a stainless-steel razor that can be refilled with new blades. Mason jars hold leftovers without a need for plastic wrap. Instead of adopting these practices simply from a sense of obligation, play with the idea that throughout the day they remind you that you are not disposable.

Second, strive each day to find someone or something or some place that has been discarded and get to know it, or them. I frequently sit on the sidewalk and break bread with people who call to me from behind their cardboard signs. Often, I invite people home to have a meal and wash up. (Living in community makes that easier . . . with ten or twenty housemates, the porch and the kitchen are still public spaces).

One day, a woman in Washington, D.C. asked me for money. I told her truthfully that I had none. I asked, "Is there anything else I can give you?" She thought about it for a while, and then said, "A hug?" We held each other until we were both crying. Finally, as she pulled away she said, "I needed that." So did I!

Take home a piece of litter tossed by the breeze and find a new purpose for it. In one class I taught, we each committed to finding a piece of trash and incorporating it into our prayer or meditation practice for a week. We stared at it for hours until we could see its beauty. We found that something shifted in us and stirred longings for reconciliation with people we had pushed out of our lives. We were re-membering that we are not whole on our own. We cannot be fully human while we continue to disown parts of ourselves and project them onto the Other, onto trash.

Find a forgotten place, a wasteland, a sacrifice zone. Dwell there.

Once I was led on a "toxic tour" of Newark, New Jersey. We came to a spot that was infamously contaminated and I heard a voice in my heart calling to me, "Take off your shoes. The place where you are standing is holy ground." I was (rather impractically) wearing sandals, and I was able to slip my feet out of them without drawing any attention. I felt the dust and sand between my toes. I noticed a layer of dirt already starting to cover my bare skin and infiltrating the cuffs of my jeans. I knew that I was breathing it, taking the finest particles of this toxic dust deep into my lungs, where it was passing into my bloodstream. The demarcation between "me" and "dust" was being erased. But not just for me. For all of us on this toxic tour, and for all—humans and others—who called this place home.

**The author traveling through the home of the Aamjiwnaang carrying the spirit of the water.**

In 2015, I went on another toxic tour, this time of the ancestral home of the Aamjiwnaang First Nation. Today this place is called Chemical Valley. Over sixty petrochemical factories and oil refineries and are clustered on fifteen square miles.[35] This time, several years of study of toxicology later, I left none of my skin bare. I breathed through a mask with a carbon filter. It didn't matter. Just as I had in Newark, I became part of the place and the place became part of me.

Try as we might, we cannot separate ourselves from the environment. No air filter or water filter or Tyvex suit is going to keep the contamination out. And try as we might, we cannot separate ourselves from each other. No gated community or border wall or zoning ordinance is really going to keep people apart. And try as we might, we cannot separate ourselves from ourselves. All of the things that we love, all of the things that we fear, and all of the things that we wish were different are still part of us, no matter what we purge.

We don't need disposability. We need authentic relationships —with all of our neighbors, with places, and with ourselves. It's all sacred.


## Friends

"I will *not* compost!" Jared bellowed, viciously stuffing his banana peel into the trash and punctuating his words with jabs at the pile of apple scraps he had hidden beneath it. "What good is it going to do anyway? You think you are going to save the world by composting?"

This is my intentional Quaker community, where we are supposed to be skilled at resolving conflicts peaceably. This is my friend.

And I didn't have a good answer for him. When I pulled out my well-reasoned response about the efficacy of individual action, he contrived a more sophisticated tack: "Why should we pay for someone to come pick up our compost? That's privatizing an ecosystem service that nature provides for free. It shouldn't be part of the cash economy."

---

35. "Chemical Valley".

I conceded defeat.

Jared had a graduate degree in economics from Tufts and had already earned enough as an actuary that, at 28, he could have retired. He certainly could have lived lavishly. Instead, he had chosen a simple room at the Beacon Hill Friends House, sharing a bathroom with four and a kitchen with twenty. He did not own a car and rarely bought what he could make for himself. In many ways, his lifestyle epitomizes the conscientious, community-minded ethos I strive to embody. People are complex. Who is my ally? Who is my enemy? What happens when they are the same person?

When Quakers feel stumped, they make up more questions, which for tradition's sake are called "queries." So, these are the questions I came up with: Why am I insisting that Jared compost? Am I making this request in order to gain control over him, or over a situation in which I otherwise feel powerless (in this case, climate change and global biodiversity loss)? Am I feeling resentful or judgmental? Am I using facts and statistics to gain power over him? To make him feel guilt or shame? To embarrass him?

Oops.

Most disconcerting, I realized that the smug, "expert" persona I was cultivating was masking a growing sense of powerlessness. I recognized that my own life was contributing to the very problems I was researching, and I had no idea how to shift that. As much as I had lectured Jared about the value of individual actions, deep down I didn't believe it anymore.

As environmentalists, we have painted ourselves into a corner where if the problem is human behavior and even human overpopulation, then the solution is for humanity to take up less and less space—or even disappear. The guiding metaphor is sacrifice, which is sold as "reducing our (carbon, water, plastics, toxic) footprint." Isn't there a way to affirm the worth inherent in all people *and* learn to take only what we need from the earth?

## DANCING RABBIT ECO-VILLAGE, OR HOW I GAVE UP ON LIVING PLASTIC-FREE

Since approximately 80 percent of plastic in the ocean comes from land-based sources, and since one of those land-based sources is me, I needed to untangle my ethical dissonance. I resolved to move to an eco-village, build a tiny cob house with no plastic; to subsist entirely on unpackaged, organic, locally grown produce; and to stop buying or using anything that involved plastic anywhere in its life cycle. Since the eco-village I chose is a demonstration project, we would give tours, host groups of visitors for longer stays, and attract attention from the press. I thought that in this way, perhaps the message that plastic-free is possible would reach a broad audience and have some meaningful impact.

My arrival was not auspicious.

Since I was moving by train, I'd taken what I couldn't carry with me to the local UPS store for packing and shipping. I had made small talk with the staff behind the counter about my project, explaining that I was committed to avoiding the use of plastic wherever possible. However, they were trained to equate foam stuffing with courtesy and professionalism—the more they wanted to project the impression that they valued my possessions, the more stuffing went into the boxes.

To my horror, when I opened a box containing only a pillow and a yoga mat (each of which had been carefully wrapped in its own plastic bag) I discovered that it was overflowing with Styrofoam peanuts. After puzzling over how a pillow and a yoga mat were deemed in need of such "protection," I headed over to find my new friends Kyle and Caleb to see if they could help me think of a use for them. Unbeknownst to me, the box was leaking.

A trail of Styrofoam(TM) peanuts soon led from my house, Bluestem, to Gobcobatron (at Dancing Rabbit, houses, like boats, have names). By the time I realized what was happening, the breeze had picked them up and was tossing them around my new neighbors' gardens. Violet, one of the children who had taken to following me around, looked up at me disapprovingly and scolded, "Sasha, did you come here to pollute my home with plastic?"

By making it a game, I enlisted the children's help in chasing down the airborne Styrofoam peanuts and collecting them into the plastic bags. Eventually it was determined that they could be used to stuff beanbag chairs for the community center. My guilt was appeased somewhat by this creative suggestion, but the lesson in humility still stung. (I've since heard that a non-toxic, biodegradable substitute for Styrofoam is being grown—Ecovative is selling mycelium or "myco foam"[36] to retailers like Dell and IKEA).

To make matters worse, my refuse alone was overflowing the capacity of the village's trash and recycling center. I climbed into the garbage dumpster and stomped around to try to compress the pieces of rigid Styrofoam that had turned up in other packages I'd received. The problem with my technique was that the more I jumped and stomped, the more tiny pieces broke off and were swept airborne. It would not squish. It would not go away.

Bigger disappointments were in store. I met with Hassan, a village resident with a talent for designing and constructing dwellings out of natural materials. I explained that I was prepared to rely on candlelight, since wiring the house for electricity (solar panels or otherwise) would require a good deal of plastic. However, it turns out that even that concession was insufficient. A living roof requires a plastic moisture barrier, else the interior becomes moldy. There is no non-plastic material that will do the job. And straw bales must be tied with synthetic rope. A natural rope would degrade too quickly and the bales would fall apart, compromising the structural integrity of the house.

Another puzzle to solve was drinking water. Cisterns that store rainwater could, in theory, be made of clay or stainless steel, but these may or may not survive the constant expansion and contraction of the ground during Missouri's freeze-and-thaw winters. If I were to carry water, I would be collecting it from a source that somewhere along the line used plastic (either someone else's cistern, or municipal water).

36. "Ikea".

The ponds on our land were not ideal for drinking, owing in part to the farmers who frequently hired pilots to aerially spray their pesticides. (If they would tell me *what* they were spraying and *when*, I might be able to calculate its half-life and determine how long to wait before drawing water, but historically they have not been forthcoming with this information.) Being a demonstration village, we didn't worry about these problems only for our own sakes. We wanted to find safe, healthy, replicable solutions that could be sustainable in other low-technology settings. We didn't ever want to offer a "solution"—especially to people who have fewer choices—that we were not willing and able to live with ourselves. This was my ideal. I failed to live up to it.

To make matters worse, I was spending way too much time on the train, commuting back and forth to conferences and visiting loved ones on the East coast. As much as I care about plastics, I also care about my budget, and not just my carbon budget. I decided to settle for making a conventional apartment as plastic-free as practically possible.

If we set aside for a moment that my spiffy plastic-free finds (unless they are second-hand) tend to come in the mail wrapped in plastic packaging, the downstream (visible to the consumer) plastic was fairly simple to eliminate. It's the upstream plastic that proves stubbornly resistant to individual decision-making, and which is in need of a major structural overhaul.

I'm still sorting through piles of ethical contradictions. My ideals, when I articulate them, are congruous. Each represents one expression of an aspiration to minimize the direct and indirect suffering that I cause. In practice, though, they too often appear antithetical. How did vegans become a prime marketing demographic for the plastics industry?

Before synthetic fibers, clothing was made of fur, leather, wool, cotton, and linen (which is made of flax). Today, we also use hemp and bamboo to make fabric. Some of the bamboo derivatives, like Tencel, skirt the line (pardon the pun) between plant and biopolymer. Of these, only fur and wool provide much warmth, but neither is acceptable within a vegan ethical framework. Is it more ethical then to opt for synthetic fleece?

Perhaps the question, "wool or fleece?" is a false dichotomy. A new type of synthetic leather is being made from the leaves of pineapples, which industry would otherwise regard as a waste product.[37] There are also insulating base layers made of bamboo. Market-driven demand has created other plastic-free vegan alternatives as well, for those who can afford them.

So what is to be done with all of the plastic that we already own? To throw it away would feed disposable culture, but what if keeping it poses a risk?

As news reports raised awareness of the dangers posed by brominated flame retardants to our endocrine and immune systems, many people of means donated their upholstered furniture to thrift shops to make room for new "eco-friendly" less-toxic models. And more people without access to resources were able to afford to bring brominated flame retardants into their homes. I have not sorted through all of the contradictions.

I did choose to give up an old childhood friend—a stuffed Jemima Puddle Duck. Jemima, whose "feathers" were made of synthetic fleece, was filled with the aforementioned synthetic foam and toxic flame retardants. When I was quite small, I ate her beak and her feet. My mother, whose self-worth hinged on having a picture-perfect home and an immaculate infant, switched it out for a new one. Number Two's beak also was soon nibbled to a nub. My mother, who made all of my baby food from scratch to avoid exposing me to salt and refined sugar, had inadvertently fed me polyurethane foam laced with toxic flame retardants. Many, many years later, when I became a (foster) parent, I determined not to let the toxic legacy repeat itself. Ducky was sent, rather unceremoniously, to the landfill. I'm still not sure that was the best solution.

In the United States where I live, some of the worst insults are "worthless" and "useless." In fact, those deemed "unproductive" (closely related to "worthless") by society at large are at risk of being denied food, shelter, and medical care in our national budgets

37. "Piñatex".

in the name of "personal responsibility." Some people are explicitly labeled as disposable ("white trash", "trailer trash", and so on); others are simply treated as if they were. The U.S. agricultural system relies heavily on the labor of migrant farm workers, many of whom are undocumented guests from Latin America. Each laborer, however indispensable, is fungible. In this system, workers are thought of as equivalent labor-units that, transportation barriers aside, can be substituted one for another. It is not new, this mentality of disposable culture.

How do we resist?

I've found that wherever I am, I need to go inward first. When I look in a mirror, do I see Christ, in one of his "many distressing disguises" as Mother Theresa once put it? Am I able to take a long, loving look at all that I am, without turning away from the parts I don't like? Otherwise, whatever I disavow in myself, I know I will end up projecting onto others. Whatever I disavow in myself, I also project onto trash. I will try to distance myself from it by throwing "away" people or things—whatever carries all these rejected/projected traits. Dirty. Worthless. Ugly. Broken. Used. Useless.

Advertisers know this. They teach us that when we possess or use soiled, dingy objects, we ourselves are unclean. Single-use disposable plastic to the rescue. Without our drive to avoid unclean things, or to avoid being mistaken for one, consumerism would cease to function.

Since my faith tradition is replete with proscriptions to separate myself from what is unclean, it is rather ironic that I still turn there to find hope. Half-hidden by all the "abominations", I find verses like 1 Samuel 16:7: "*The Lord does not look at the things people look at. People look at the outward appearance, but the Lord looks at the heart.*"

How do I learn to see through outward appearances, of people and of things, into the heart? Otherwise, how will I ever recognize God, who is likened in Isaiah 53 to a weed: "...a scrawny seedling, a scrubby plant in a parched field. There was nothing attractive about him, nothing to cause us to take a second look. He was looked down on and passed over, a man who suffered, who knew pain firsthand. One look at him and people turned away. We looked down on him, thought he was scum." This same God who, in my story, came to us disguised as a marginalized person from a backwater village, who ate with and befriended mostly those society had labeled trash. *"The stone which the builders had rejected has become the chief cornerstone. This is God's doing, and it is wonderful in our eyes."*

In this lonely and broken world, where do I look for God? I chose to start in the trash pile.

# 4

## Conclusion: Solutions

PUBLIC HEALTH SPEAKS OF three types of prevention. Primary prevention keeps people from experiencing injury or illness in the first place. Secondary prevention aims to diagnose problems early in the hope that prompt treatment will improve the chance of a cure. Tertiary prevention is a set of mitigation strategies that are designed to decrease symptoms and to facilitate adaptation to the new-normal impairment. So we have an emphasis on a healthy diet and sufficient exercise as primary prevention, mammograms for early detection of breast cancer as an example of secondary prevention, and occupational therapy following an amputation as one type of tertiary prevention. What would this framework look like if applied to the world's plastic problem?

I would liken the burgeoning science of quantifying microplastics in seawater, foodstuffs, tap water, and puddles to secondary prevention. We are diagnosing a problem that already exists and assessing the extent of the damage. Post-consumer recycling, finding microbes to eat our trash, and launching enormous drift nets to capture ocean waste could only be called tertiary prevention. They are not a cure; they merely mitigate the symptoms and help us adapt to a new-normal diseased state. What, then, of primary prevention?

### TERTIARY PREVENTION: CLEAN IT UP

As discussed in the preceding chapter on environmental justice, sometimes "clean up" projects function to euphemistically mask moving a problem from one place to another, or from one media to another (solid waste being burned and creating air pollution, for example), or from one generation to another. I term these displacement across space, displacement across media, and displacement across time. In some instances, however, remediation techniques do exist to degrade plastic completely into its atomic-level building blocks, rendering it once again non-toxic.

As previously described, mealworm larvae and some types of fungi have been observed to digest and degrade plastics. While promising, these novel trophic relationships raise questions. Given the abundance of plastic waste we provide them, these tiny creatures have a marked advantage over their counterparts who thrive on plant matter, potentially shifting the composition of the ecosystem. If we raise these specialists in the laboratory for release into landfills, which in turn release them into the soil and groundwater, will there be unintended consequences for the existing biota?

Meanwhile, we busy ourselves moving waste around rather than detoxifying it. Small-scale cleanup projects are often organized by environmental advocacy groups and by state and federal entities such as, in the United States, the National Oceanographic and Aeronautic Administration (NOAA). Volunteers collect macro-plastics, preventing them from becoming microplastic contamination. The garbage is moved from waterways and from coastal habitats to landfills, or in some cases, to incinerators. Volunteers may take home increased awareness and a sense of ownership of the problem that leads them to change their own behavior and to educate others.

Ironically, we have delegated some of this labor to automated plastic devices, such as the Seabin: a "floating debris interception device" marketed for deployment at marinas and other coastal hotspots. It is constructed of plastic mesh and relies on a 110/22 volt motor. It can capture up to 1.5 kilograms of plastic debris per day under ideal conditions.[1]

Others aim to clean up the plastic dispersed at sea. Among these initiatives, Boyan Slat's Ocean Cleanup is the most ambitious. It aims to collect half of the plastic from the North Pacific "garbage patch" within five years using an energy-neutral system of

1. "Seabin Project".

one to two-kilometer-long polypropylene floats attached to massive screens that will follow the same currents as the debris, slowed by drift anchors. The collected trash will be brought to shore for recycling.[2] This will capture the neustonic (floating) plastic larger than one centimeter, but not smaller pieces or pieces submerged below the catchment area of the screens.

The success of marine debris removal projects, however, is entirely dependent on upstream source reduction. That is, as long as we continue to add the equivalent of one full garbage truck full of plastic to the ocean *each minute*,[3] our efforts to skim it off will be in vain. For this reason, I have affectionately nicknamed him Boyan "Sisyphus" Slat, after the Greek myth of the man forced to endlessly push a huge boulder uphill. No sooner does he reach the top than the boulder rolls back down and the process begins again. For me, this is a cautionary tale that working alone—no matter our strength or determination—we are bound to fail. Instead, if we allow Boyan's vision and contagious optimism to inspire us to keep new plastic out of production, he just might succeed.

## More Tertiary Prevention: Reduce, Reuse, Recycle

Many individuals, groups, and some companies have taken steps to reduce their use of disposable plastic. At the level of individual behavioral change, I am an admirer of Beth Terry, author of *Plastic-Free: How I Kicked the Plastic Habit and How You Can Too* and blogger at *https://myplasticfreelife.com*. We can follow her lead and commit to "#StopSucking"[4] (to refrain from using disposable straws) or take the Plastic Pollution Coalition's 4R Pledge.[5] However, as we brush with bamboo toothbrushes, using tooth powder from a glass jar, we are probably still standing in a building sided with vinyl, with vinyl windows, and probably vinyl flooring. The

2. "Ocean Cleanup".
3. Pennington, "Every Minute".
4. "For a Strawless Ocean".
5. "Plastic Pollution Coalition".

toilet seat and shower curtain are more than likely also plastic, as are the pipes that drain the water from the sink and the tub, and as are the jackets around the wires that bring electricity to the bathroom light. Most of the plastic we use is invisible to us or is not there by our choosing.

I was browsing the fresh produce section at Whole Foods when I spotted an employee stacking organic eggplant. Each was in an individual plastic sleeve, which he was busy removing before adding the eggplant to the display. I asked him how many "unpackaged" fruits and vegetables arrive at the store wrapped in plastic but his answer was an evasive, "I don't know." There has been no reply to my e-mail to corporate headquarters. This underscores the importance of demanding transparency and of acting collectively in addition to (*not instead of*) making our own lifestyle changes.

Just as individuals can take a public pledge to reduce their plastic use,[6] corporations too can publicly quantify their plastic footprint at the Plastic Disclosure Project.[7] Fabricators can follow best practices to minimize their nurdle[8] loss by following the guidelines set forth in Operation Clean Sweep.[9] Some companies are experimenting with laser etching instead of plastic tags on loose bananas[10] and avocados.[11] The cosmetics company Lush has a line of "naked" shampoo bars, soap bars, toothpaste tablets, and other cosmetics sold without any packaging. Patagonia bears mention as well for their investment in evaluating the damage that microfibers shed from their synthetic garments do and in seeking ways to mitigate it.[12] Avasol is pioneering non-toxic sunscreens packaged

---

6. "Pledges Galore".

7. "Plastic Disclosure Project".

8. Nurdles, also called mermaid's tears, are pre-fabrication plastic resin pellets.

9. "Operation Clean Sweep".

10. Pullman, "Swedish Supermarkets".

11. Butler, "Tattooing".

12. Patagonia, "Update".

without any plastic.[13] Sky, a European satellite broadcaster, has committed to not using single-use plastics at all by 2020.[14]

These forms of use reduction, or "source reduction," are preferred over finding ways to recycle plastic. The use of the term "recycling" in reference to plastics is contentious. Rarely can a plastic be reformed in a closed loop into the same sort of object again and again. Instead it is typically "up-cycled" into art, or "down-cycled" into a less technically demanding application. For example, one of the few uses of post-consumer polyethylene film (such as single-use plastic bags) is being incorporated into Trex,[15] a wood substitute. Polyethylene terephthalate bottles often become fleece. This postpones the problem of the ultimate disposal of the plastic only as long as the Trex or fleece product is in use. Still, there are encouraging examples of downcycling. Hewlett Packard has stated an intention to decouple business growth from materials consumption. Towards this end, they are working with THREAD in Haiti to collect plastic bottles that can be turned into ink cartridges. Because the ink cartridges are black, its producers, unlike most, can accept bottles in a mix of colors.[16]

To complicate matters, incorporating post-consumer plastic into a product tends to be more costly and complex than using a fresh batch, with unstable supply chains posing even more complications. The international market for plastic recycling is volatile, and as of this writing, China's "National Sword 2017" initiative, increasing enforcement of the 2013 "Operation Green Fence" rules, has sharply limited the quality of material that Chinese (re-) processors will be allowed to accept, leaving some U.S. recycling companies renting warehouse space to store their sorted plastics in hopes of a near-future return to a more relaxed market.[17] This

13. "Avasol".
14. Moore, "Sky to Remove".
15. Paben, "End User".
16. "HP Announces".
17. Paben, "China".

is already having dramatic effects on municipal curbside recycling programs.[18]

For these reasons, a study by the United Kingdom-based circular-economy focused nonprofit Ellen MacArthur Foundation estimates that just 14 percent of the world's plastic packaging is collected for recycling, and of that, only 2 percent goes toward a closed-loop system. Eight percent is downcycled, and the remaining 4 percent is diverted back into the regular waste stream.[19]

Industry frequently laments that the plastic problem would be solved if consumers would simply dispose of plastic waste "responsibly." However, the infrastructure is not ready to accommodate it. In the UK, 2.5 billion disposable "paper" coffee cups are used each year, but since they are lined with plastic, even those sorted into recycling bins are ultimately rerouted to landfills or incineration. The plastic lining complicates the recycling process and requires specialized machinery, which is not widely available. Only 1 percent of these cups are actually recycled.[20] Encouraging customers to bring in a reusable travel mug to be filled would be an alternative; however, there would need to be infrastructure to sanitize reusable containers and cups to avoid a different sort of public health problem.[21]

## SECONDARY PREVENTION: MEASURE THE MESS

There is often an overlap between research and teaching, by design. Citizen science itself can be viewed as a form of popular education. Hideshige Takada, a professor at the Tokyo University of Agriculture and Technology and founder of the International Pellet Watch program, is engaging citizen scientists in collecting pellets along beaches throughout the world, which Takada then analyzes for POPs. This project of synthesizing data that quantifies

18. "Oregon Refuse".
19. "New Plastics"
20. Taylor, "Coffee Shops".
21. Dennis, "Shopping Bag".

the contaminants of interest in the water matrix and biota is intended as a first step towards understanding the movement of contaminants through the food web. Another example is Five Gyres, TrawlShare program. This makes the equipment necessary to sample at sea available at no cost.

Governments could be more involved in this endeavor. Now that micro – and nanoplastics have been widely detected in tap water,[22] the U.S. Geological Survey should consider adding this testing parameter to its data collection.[23] The National Health and Nutrition Examination Survey (NHANES), which collects biospecimens and survey data from thousands of volunteers in a nationally representative sample, should begin testing for microplastics and nanoplastics in human serum and urine.[24]

## Using Plastics to Purify

Ironically, polymers themselves may be a useful tool in understanding our "exposome." Dr. Kim Anderson has created a silicone bracelet that records, so to speak, any of 1,200 chemical compounds that the wearer's wrist comes into contact with—either in water (from showering, swimming, or precipitation) or in the air. This does not, of course, take into account anything that the wearer ate, or personal care products (such as makeup) that did not touch the bracelet. It is being used now to track the exposures of residents in Texas following the Hurricane Harvey-related flooding of toxic waste sites.[25]

The bracelet itself is inexpensive; the chemical extraction of the contaminants it holds, however, costs thousands of dollars, putting it out of reach of unfunded citizen scientists. Another disadvantage is that because it utilizes a targeted approach, we only

---

22. Morrison and Tyree, "Invisibles".
23. "USGS Current Water Data".
24. "National Health and Nutrition Examination Survey".
25. O'Connell et al., "Silicone Wristbands", 3327–3335.

find what we are looking for. Still, it could archive our exposome for future research when we know different questions to ask.

Because of this lipophilicity, plastics can pollute, and plastics can also purify. Polystyrene and other synthetic polymers are used in ion-exchange media to filter such varied liquids as drinking water, fruit juices (to remove bitter flavors), and biodiesel. The resin beads can capture lead and cadmium, replacing them with sodium and potassium. "Bio-beads" are already used, though not widely, in the UK in water filtration plants.[26] There are concerns about wastewater treatment plants themselves becoming sources of microplastics via these fugitive beads, however, and hopefully a safe method of rinsing and reusing the beads will be developed.

## POLICY AND REGULATORY SOLUTIONS: A MIXED BAG

Costa Rica has declared that it will develop a plan over the next four years to end its use of all forms of disposable plastic.[27] The Indian state of Karnataka has banned not only all forms of plastic carry bags, but also plastic banners, buntings, flex, flags, plates, cups, spoons, cling films and plastic tablecloths.[28] Sikkim, India, has also banned expanded polystyrene food containers, with an exemption for milk products.[29] As of 2020, any disposable cutlery, plates, or cups used in France will be required to break down in home compost bins to be at least 50 percent biologically sourced.[30] More than twelve U.S. cities have implemented a complete or partial ban on polystyrene, although some of these are being challenged in court.[31]

26. Taylor, "Sewage Plants".
27. Gutiérrez, "Costa Rica".
28. Moudgal, "Total Plastic".
29. Ibid.
30. Ellsbury, "France".
31. MacEachern, "Styrofoam".

Several countries have joined the UNEP's Clean Seas campaign, including Belgium, Brazil, Canada, Costa Rica, France, Grenada, Indonesia, Italy, Madagascar, the Maldives, Norway, Panama, Peru, Saint Lucia, Sierra Leone, and Uruguay.[32]The European Union as a whole, however, has ruled out penalties on single-use plastic products, in favor of raising public awareness of the damage consumer plastics are doing to the world's oceans.[33]

By 2021, the world will produce half a trillion single-use plastic bottles each year.[34] Coca-Cola™ alone produces 110 billion bottles each year, according to Greenpeace (one billion more this year than last).[35] Only 3 percent of all plastic bottles were collected for recycling and turned into new bottles. Recognizing the danger, over eighty schools, colleges, and universities have forbidden the sale of bottled water on their campuses.[36] Instead, they offer free filtered water at bottle refill stations and drinking fountains. Some towns and cities in Australia, Canada, India, and the United States have banned bottled water with various exceptions.[37] A short-lived ban on bottled water in US national parks was estimated to have prevented the waste of between 1.32 and 2 million plastic water bottles annually before the Trump administration rescinded the ban.[38]

New Zealand, Australia, UK, Canada, Taiwan, and the United States have banned microbeads in personal care products, and several other countries are considering such legislation.[39]

Disposable shopping bags are one of the most frequently regulated uses of plastic. In Bangladesh, the first nation to enact a ban, concerns were centered not on marine debris but on the problem

32. "United Nations Declares War"; "Clean Seas."
33. Harvey, "EU Rules".
34. Laville and Taylor, "Million Bottles".
35. Laville , "Coca-Cola".
36. "Map of Campaigns".
37. "Bottled Water Ban".
38. "Disposable Plastic Water Bottle".
39. Lai, "Taiwan".

of clogged drains, which increase the likelihood of flooding.[40] Littered plastic bags also pool water, creating new breeding sites for mosquitoes.[41] Nearly forty countries have followed Bangladesh's lead; however, lax enforcement reduces the impact in many parts of the world. While the United States, Canada, Australia, Argentina, and Malaysia have no national regulations, many local, state, and provincial governments have imposed bans or fines.[42] However, Michigan, Arizona, Idaho, Minnesota, Iowa, Missouri, Wisconsin, Florida and Indiana have passed legislation *preventing* local governments in their states from regulating plastic bags.[43]

## BIOPLASTICS: MOVING TOWARDS PRIMARY PREVENTION?

*Bio-derived plastics* are chemically indistinguishable from their petrochemical counterparts. It does not matter whether the constituent carbon and hydrogen atoms were extracted from plants or from oil. Once they are mixed with oxygen and rearranged into long chains of bis(2-hydroxyethyl) terephthalate, they have exactly the same toxic properties as do the conventionally manufactured monomers, and in all likelihood use the same problematic additives as do conventional plastics, conferring no environmental advantages at the disposal stage. An example of this is the blend of PET used in Coca-Cola's "Plant Bottle™".[44]

Some, however, use natural materials to create an entirely different monomer, such as polyethylene furanoate (PEF).[45] If the toxic petrochemical additives are not used, and if it biodegrades (not all bioplastic is biodegradable), then we are moving back towards materials borrowed from nature. There has been con-

---

40. Admin., "Bangladesh"; "Polythene Choking Drains".
41. Traore, "Gender".
42. "List by Country"; "Phase-out"; Riskey, "Which Countries".
43. "State Plastic".
44. "Plant Bottle".
45. Gotro, "Polyethylene Furanoate".

cern about using plants for plastic that would otherwise be used for food. In response, researchers are making some bioplastics from bacteria. One example is polyhydroxyalkanoates (PHAs).[46] Then there are the truly innovative solutions: "Ooho," an edible water bottle, is made of a simple seaweed and calcium chloride membrane.[47]

Compostable/biodegradable plastics are another active front for research, albeit one rife with dubious claims that border on greenwashing. One example is the blending of conventional plastic with starch to give the illusion that it breaks down in a compost bin. In reality, the starch breaks down, leaving tiny pieces of plastic invisible to the naked eye, but all the more easily ingested by unwary organisms. If these organisms do not digest it but merely carry it within their bodies, then it may accumulate in its predators as well, introducing yet another pathway for plastics to concentrate in the food web. Other compostable plastics, such as polylactide (PLA) and polybutylene adipate terephthalate (PBAT), have been blamed for contaminating the recycling stream and rendering bales of conventional post-consumer plastic worthless.[48]

Nevertheless, Saudi Arabia and the United Arab Emirates, among other nations, have mandated that polypropylene and polyethylene for use in non-durable goods (though packaging is excepted)[49] be modified with a petrochemical-derived oxo-biodegradable catalyst that speeds the end-of-life decomposition of (otherwise conventional) plastics.[50] It does this by breaking the high-molecular weight polymeric chains into lower-weight molecules. However, a coalition of 150 groups, from industry to environmental advocacy organizations, have signed on to the Ellen MacArthur Foundation's New Plastics Economy initiative to call for a ban of these additives, arguing that they create more

46. European Bioplastics e.v. "Highlights".
47. Skipping Rocks Lab, "Ooho!".
48. Stephen, "Consider the Benefit".
49. Giger, "New Regulations".
50. Oxobiodegradable Plastics Association, "Preventing Oceans".

environmental problems than they solve.[51] For example, when consumers believe that a product will degrade "more quickly than a leaf,"[52] as the promotional materials promise, they are more likely to litter than to bother with putting it into a trash or recycling bin.[53]

## PRIMARY PREVENTION

A primary prevention approach that addresses the root causes would involve not only technological advances but a new worldview. Our task is not necessarily to imagine a world without plastics, but a world without disposable plastics—and without the habits of instrumentalism that they signify.

Plastics are accelerating the commodification of the planet. Twenty-six percent of all plastic (311 million tons in 2014) is used for packaging.[54] We are told that this serves to protect our products, and to extend their shelf life,[55] in some cases rather dramatically, which is all quite true. However, it is also true that much of this packaging is devoted simply to advertising and branding—and this is where a great deal of industry's profits are to be made. Only 15 percent of the price of cosmetics, for example, represents the cost of the ingredients.[56] The rest is for "marketing, packaging, and branding,"[57] and the line of demarcation between these is fuzzy indeed.

Packaging signifies that an item has become a commodity. Until it is bottled and stamped with a brand logo, water does not seem to belong to anyone. It doesn't make much sense to sell it

51. Staub, "Diverse Group".

52. "Nature's wastes such as leaves twigs and straw may take ten years or more to biodegrade, but oxo-bio plastics will biodegrade more quickly than that, and much more quickly than ordinary plastic." (Oxobiodegradable Plastics Association, "Standards").

53. "Impact of the Use of 'Oxo-Degradable' Plastic."

54. *The New Plastics Economy*

55. Tullo, "Cost".

56. Bryant, "Here's Why".

57. Ibid.

(unless you are selling the infrastructure used to deliver it, as is the case with municipal water utilities). Once it has become Evian or Fiji water, however, it can be sold for up to two thousand times the price of tap water.[58] In the past, explorers from colonizing nations planted a flag to assert possession of a territory.[59] Today we use a plastic bar code sticker.

Of course, plastics are not the first material to be used for this purpose. In the past, however, the materials used for packaging were either borrowed from nature, such as cornhusks or banana leaves, or were on loan to the consumer. The market value of glass bottles and metal cans incentivized, and continues to incentivize, their collection, sterilization, and reuse. In the case of most cheap plastic packaging, virtually no one has an interest in reclaiming it.

Today, half of all plastic produced is intended to be single-use/disposable.[60] And there is quite a bit of it. As of July 2017, 8,300 million metric tons of plastic have been produced, of which only two thousand million metric tons are still in use. Seventy-nine percent of the spent 6,300 million metric tons is already in landfills or littering the natural environment.[61] Twelve percent has been burned, and nine percent has been recycled, delaying its inevitable disposal.[62]

In order to create a society where no one and no-thing is wasted, we will need a fundamental shift in our relationships. Astrid Ulloa calls for a relational indigenous environmental justice that is:

> ". . . based on a sense of responsibility and reciprocity . . . putting relational ontologies at the center of a rights-based approach to consider nonhumans' rights, including to not forget the implications of epistemic violence and ethno – and ecocide generated by the current global

58. Boesler, "Bottled Water".

59. I cannot resist pointing out that today almost all flags are plastic (either polyester or nylon).

60. Hopewell et al., "Plastics Recycling", 2115–26.

61. Geyer et al., "Production".

62. Ibid.

environmental geopolitics of knowledge and economic dynamics; proposing other notions of justice by including territory and "nature" as "victims" of processes of extractions and destruction of environment; considering historical inequalities that were respondent to modern dual conceptions, which were implemented since the conquest and colonial processes; confronting the extractivist processes that erased legal, environmental, and cultural rights previously recognized; and demanding other perspectives of environmental justice in which humans, nonhumans, and the territory are included as living beings and as political actors."[63]

Ulloa reminds us that some people and some ecosystems have been treated as disposable long before commodity plastics entered the scene.

Fundamentally, plastic marine debris and terrestrial plastic litter do not bother us because it is unsightly or even because it is toxic. Collectively, far fewer voices protest other unsightly and toxic situations like Agbogbloshie or Chemical Valley in Sarnia. No, we protest because plastic wastelands hold up a mirror that reflects what we do not want to see in ourselves. Plastics were going to protect rare species from poaching, by offering an alternative to ivory. Plastics were supposed to democratize. Luxury goods, or at least facsimiles thereof, would be mass produced and available to all. Plastics were supposed to reduce drudgery. Instead of washing dishes, some of us could simply toss them in the bin. We thought that they made us modern and free.

Instead, they remind us that the world of abundance and luxury that we have created is merely an illusion. Rejecting 侘寂 wabi-sabi—the beauty of imperfection and impermanence—we hold ourselves to the same low standards that we do our mass-produced goods. We imagine that we, too, should be functional, uniform, and without any distinguishing blemishes.

We are reminded when children mouth their plastic toys that they are taking in more than marketing and early socialization. They might be swallowing chemicals that reduce their chances

63. Ulloa, "Perspectives", 175–80.

of someday starting a biological family of their own. That these chemicals, having initiated harm that may take decades to manifest, will pass through their bodies and into the watershed. That they will go on to harm many, many, more, perhaps for centuries to come.

To make matters worse, someone else's child choked on the fumes from the petroleum distillate, naphtha, that was "cracked" into ethylene and mixed with chlorine to produce the sickly sweet-smelling vinyl chloride monomer that became the toy. Someone else's child might have made this toy, earning 0.016 US cents, which is 1/2000th of the price it sells for.[64] Someday someone else's child might come across that toy as they sort through mountains of garbage, earning between five and twenty-three cents a kilogram for the resalable or recyclable plastic they find.[65] They would toss it aside. Post-consumer PVC has no value in the modern economy. Nor does the waste picker.

That waste picker, who earns less than two dollars a day, cannot afford soap or cooking oil. They purchase it, one single-use portion at a time, in little plastic pouches. And some Western environmental activists blame them and the "sachet economy" they "support" for the plastic scraps that scatter in the wind, burying the reclaimable pieces that mound in ever-higher piles in the dump.

The world we are creating is incompatible with life. We have devised an economic system that would collapse if people's real needs were met. Insatiable greed is slaked in single-serving portions that come individually wrapped in plastic.

We are better than that . . . aren't we?

64. "For instance, in 2007 more than 300 middle school students, some child labor under 16, were discovered toiling 11 hours a day at a plastic toy factory. Several students' health suffered as a result of long hours and chemical poisoning; one female student even died." (China Labor Watch, "Other Side".)

65. Ocean Conservancy, *Stemming the Tide.*

# Bibliography

"Aamjiwnaang First Nation." *Canada First Nations* (January 2014). www.first-nations.info/aamjiwnaang-first-nation.html.

Admin. "Bangladesh: World Leader in Banning the Plastic Bag." *Greenpage* (June 2013).greenpagebd.net/bangladesh-world-leader-in-banning-the-plastic-bag/.

"Amberlite® GT73 hydrogen form." https://www.sigmaaldrich.com/catalog/product/supelco/10354?lang=en&region=US.

Andersson, M.A., et al. "Boar Spermatozoa as a Biosensor for Detecting Toxic Substances in Indoor Dust and Aerosols." *Toxicology in Vitro* 24 (2010) 2041–52.

Ashton, Karen, et al. "Association of Metals with Plastic Production Pellets in the Marine Environment." *Marine Pollution Bulletin* 60 (2010) 2050–55.

Auman, Heidi J., et al. "Plastic Ingestion by Laysan Albatross Chicks on Sand Island, Midway Atoll, in 1994 and 1995." *Albatross Biology and Conservation* (1997) 239–44.

"Avasol". http://avasol.com.

Ayitey, Charles. "Rice Producers In China Exposed For Exporting Plastic Rice." *Yen* (2015). yen.com.gh/24973-rice-producers-china-exposed-exporting-fake-rice-made-plastic-ghana-countries.html#24973.

Bennett, Mary Payne, and Cecile Lengacher. "Humor and Laughter May Influence Health IV. Humor and Immune Function." *Evidence-based Complementary and Alternative Medicine: eCAM* 6.2 (2009) 159–64.

Besseling, Ellen, et al. "Nanoplastic Affects Growth of *S. obliquus* and Reproduction of *D. magna*." *Environmental Science & Technology* 48 (2014) 12336–43.

Betts, Kellyn S. "Phthalates in Prescription Drugs: Some Medications Deliver High Doses." *Environmental Health Perspectives* 117 (February 2009) A74.

Biedermann-Brem, S., et al. "Release of Bisphenol A from Polycarbonate Baby Bottles: Mechanisms of Formation and Investigation of Worst Case Scenarios." *European Food Research and Technology* 227 (2008) 1053–60.

Biello, David. "Indoor Air Alert: Ozone Reacts with Human Skin to Produce Potential Irritants." *Scientific American* (August 2009). https://www.scientificamerican.com/article/ozone-reacts-with-human-skin-to-produce-irritants/.

Bilbrey, Jenna. "BPA-Free Plastic Containers May Be Just as Hazardous." *Scientific American* (August 2014). https://www.scientificamerican.com/article/bpa-free-plastic-containers-may-be-just-as-hazardous/

Biró, A., et al. "Lymphocyte Phenotype Analysis and Chromosome Aberration Frequency of Workers Occupationally Exposed to Styrene, Benzene, Polycyclic Aromatic Hydrocarbons or Mixed Solvents." *Immunology Letter* 81 (2002) 133–40.

"Bisphenol A Metabolism: Pharmacokinetic Studies Key Findings." www.bisphenol- a.org/human/herMetabolism.html#4.

"Blissfully Unaware of Bisphenol A." *Friends of the Earth Europe* (July 2008). http://www.foeeurope.org/safer_chemicals/Blissfully_unaware_of_BPA_report.pdf.

Boehler, Patrick. "Bad Eggs: Another Fake-Food Scandal Rocks China." *Time* (November 2012). newsfeed.time.com/2012/11/06/how-to-make-a-rotten-egg/.

Boesler, Matthew. "Bottled Water Costs 2000 Times As Much As Tap Water." *Business Insider* (July 2013). www.businessinsider.com/bottled-water-costs-2000x-more-than- tap-2013-7.

Boffey, Daniel. "EU Declares War on Plastic Waste." *The Guardian* (January 2018). https://www.theguardian.com/environment/2018/jan/16/eu-declares-war-on-plastic-waste-2030

"Bottled Water Ban." https://en.wikipedia.org/wiki/Bottled_water_ban.

Braun, Joe M., et al. "Variability and Predictors of Urinary Bisphenol A Concentrations During Pregnancy." *Environmental Health Perspectives* 119 (2011) 131.

Brown, S.G. and Lokyer, C.H. "Whales." In *Antarctic Ecology* 717–81. London: Academic Press, 1984.

Bryant, Taylor. "Here's Why Your Expensive Makeup Is So Expensive." *Refinery 29* (November 2015). www.refinery29.com/2015/11/96885/high-makeup-cost-explained.

Butler, Sarah. "Tattooing Avocados Helps Keep up Supply of Smash Hit." *The Guardian* (June 2017). www.theguardian.com/lifeandstyle/2017/jun/23/tattooing-avocados-helps-keep-up- supply-of-smash-hit.

Carlton, James T., et al. "Tsunami-Driven Rafting: Transoceanic Species Dispersal and Implications for Marine Biogeography." *Science* 357 (2017) 1402–06.

Carter, Lucy. "Researchers Accidently Find Industrial Waste, Orange Peel Material Sucks Mercury out of Water." *The World Today* (October 2015). www.abc.net.au/news/2015-10-19/researchers-discover-a-way-to-remove-mercury-from-water/6865462.

"CFR - Code of Federal Regulations Title 21. Sec. 173.25, Sec. 173.21, Sec. 173.20." (August 2017). www.accessdata.fda.gov/scripts/cdrh/cfdocs/cfcfr/CFRSearch.cfm?CFRPart=173&sh owFR=1&subpartNode=21:3.0.1.1.4.1%20(9/27/17).

"The chemical valley." *Vice* (August 2013). https://www.vice.com/en_us/article/4w7gwn/the-chemical-valley-part-1.

Chiarle, S., et al. "Mercury Removal from Water by Ion Exchange Resins Adsorption." *Water Research* 34 (2000) 2971–78.

"Child mortality rate drops by a third since 1990." *UNICEF Press Centre*. https://www.unicef.org/media/media_56045.html

China Labor Watch. "The Other Side of Fairy Tales: An Investigation of Labor Conditions at Five Chinese Toy Factories." (November 2015). http://www.chinalaborwatch.org/report/111

Christophersen, C. T., et al. "In vitro Methane Emission and Acetate:Propionate Ratio are Decreased When Artificial Stimulation of the Rumen Wall Is Combined With Increasing Grain Diets in Sheep." *Journal of Animal Science* 86 (2008) 384–89.

"Clean Seas." http://cleanseas.org/take-action.

Cohen, John. "Plastics Ingredient Scrambles Chromosomes." *Science* (April 2003). www.sciencemag.org/news/2003/04/plastics-ingredient-scrambles-chromosomes.

Cole, Matthew, et al. "The Impact of Polystyrene Microplastics on Feeding, Function and Fecundity in the Marine Copepod *Calanus helgolandicus.*"*Environmental Science & Technology* 49 (2015) 1130–37.

———."Microplastics Alter the Properties and Sinking Rates of Zooplankton Faecal Pellets." *Environmental Science & Technology* 50 (2016) 3239–46.

Cone, Marla. "Prescription Drugs Can Deliver High Doses of Phthalates." *Environmental Health News* (November 2008). www.ehn.org.

"Critical Windows of Development Timeline." https://endocrinedisruption.org/interactive-tools/critical-windows-of-development/view-the-timeline/. accessed 9/28/17.

"Cross-Linked Polyurethanes as Adhesive Layers for Food Packaging Materials." Germany, Bundesinstitut fur Risikobewertung/Federal Institute for Risk Assessment. bfr.ble.de/kse/faces/resources/pdf/280-english.pdf.

Dellinger, Drew. "Dr. King's Interconnected World." *The New York Times* (December 2017). https://www.nytimes.com/2017/12/22/opinion/martin-luther-king-christmas.html.

Dennis, Tami. "What's in Your Shopping Bag? Bacteria." *Chicago Tribune* (June 2010). www.chicagotribune.com/goo/lifestyles/health/sns-green-bacteria-in-shopping-bags-story.html?i10c.encReferrer=aHR0cHM6Ly9 3d3cuZ29vZ2xlLmNvbS8%3D.

Derriak, J.G.B. "The Pollution of the Marine Environment by Plastic Debris: a Review." *Marine Pollution Bulletin* 44 (2002) 842–52.

"DES Sons." https://www.cdc.gov/des/consumers/sons/.

"Disposable Plastic Water Bottle Recycling and Reduction Program Evaluation Report."

National Park Service, US Department of the Interior, Park Facility Management Division (May 2017). www.nps.gov/aboutus/foia/upload/Disposable-Plastic-Water-Bottle- Evaluation-Report_5_11_17.pdf.

Doward, Jamie. "How Did That Get There? Plastic Chunks on Arctic Ice Show How Far Pollution Has Spread." *The Guardian* (September 2017). www.theguardian.com/world/2017/sep/24/arctic-plastic-pollution-polystyrene-wildlife-threat.

EFSA Contam Panel (EFSA Panel on Contaminants in the Food Chain). "Statement on the Presence of Microplastics and Nanoplastics in Food, with Particular Focus on Seafood."*EFSA Journal* 14 (2016) 4501–31.

Ellison Rodgers, Joann. *Sex: A Natural History*. New York: Times Books, 2001.

Ellsbury, Hannah. "France Bids Adieu to Plastic Cups, Plates, and Cutlery." (November 2016). https://www.banthebottle.net/news/france-bids-adieu-to-plastic-cups-plates-and-cutlery/.

Embry, Paige. "Building a Backup Bee." *The Food and Environment Reporting Network* (February 2018). https://thefern.org/2018/02/building-backup-bee/.

"Endocrine Disruptors." Emory School of Medicine Department of Pediatrics. www.pediatrics.emory.edu/centers/pehsu/concern/disruptor.html.

Eriksen, M., et al. "Nature of Plastic Marine Pollution in the Subtropical Gyres." In *The Handbook of Environmental Chemistry*. Berlin: Springer, 2016.

"Ethylene Oxide." *Report on Carcinogens, Fourteenth Edition*. https://ntp.niehs.nih.gov/ntp /roc/content/profiles/ethyleneoxide.pdf

European Bioplastics e.V. "These Were the Highlights That Shaped Bioplastics in 2016." https://www.european-bioplastics.org/these-were-the-highlights-that-shaped-bioplastics-in-2016/

European Society of Endocrinology. "Exposure to Chemicals in Plastic and Fungicides May Irreversibly Weaken Children's Teeth." *Science Daily* (May 2016). www.sciencedaily.com/releases/2016/05/160530190144.htm.

"Exposome and Exposomics." https://www.cdc.gov/niosh/topics/exposome/default.html.

Fedak, Kristen M., et al. "Applying the Bradford Hill Criteria in the 21st Century: How Data Integration Has Changed Causal Inference in Molecular Epidemiology." *Emerging Themes in Epidemiology* 12 (2015) 14.

"Flavorings-Related Lung Disease." https://www.cdc.gov/niosh/topics/flavorings./

Fondeur, F.F., et al. "Mercury Removal Performance of Amberlite GT-73A, Purolite S-920, Ionac SR-4 and SIR-200 Resins." *Westinghouse Savannah River Company* (2002). https://clu- in.org/download/contaminantfocus/mercury/DOE_Amberlite.pdf.

"For a Strawless Ocean." https://www.strawlessocean.org/.

Freudiger H., et al. "Acroosteolysis and Raynaud's Phenomenon After Vinyl Chloride Exposure." *Vasa* 17 (1988) 216–218.

Fung, Karen, et al. "Impact of Air Pollution on Hospital Admissions in Southwestern Ontario, Canada: Generating Hypotheses in Sentinel High-Exposure Places." *Environmental Health* 6 (2007) 18.

Galloway, Tamara S. "Micro- and Nano-plastics and Human Health." In *Marine Anthropogenic Litter*, 343–66). Springer, Cham, 2015.

Garner, Rochelle, and Dafna Kohen. "Changes in the Prevalence of Asthma among Canadian Children." *Health Reports* 19 (2008) 45–50.

Gasperi, Johnny, et al. "First Overview of Microplastics in Indoor and Outdoor Air." *15th EuCheMS International Conference on Chemistry and the Environment*, 2015. HAL Archives Ouvertes. https://hal-enpc.archives-ouvertes.fr/hal-01195546.

Geyer, Roland, et al. "Production, Use, and Fate of All Plastics Ever Made." *Science Advances* 3 (2017) E1700782.

Giger, Silvana. "New Regulations for Plastics in Saudi Arabia." *Switzerland Global Enterprise* (December 2017). www.s-ge.com/en/article/news/20173-saudi-arabia-clean- plastic-legislation.

Gjerde, Kristina M. *Ecosystems and Biodiversity in Deep Waters and High Seas. UNEP Regional Seas Reports and Studies No. 178.* Switzerland: UNEP/IUCN, 2006.

Gotro, Jeffrey. "Polyethylene Furanoate (PEF): 100% Biobased Polymer to Compete with PET?" (April 2013). https://polymerinnovationblog.com/polyethylene-furanoate-pef-100-biobased-polymer-to-compete-with-pet/

Grandjean, Philippe, et al. "Life-Long Implications of Developmental Exposure to Environmental Stressors: New Perspectives." *Endocrinology* 2016 (2016) 10–16.

Gutiérrez, Edgar. "Costa Rica Paves the Way to End Single-Use Plastics." United Nations Development Program (July 2017). www.undp.org/content/undp/en/home/blog/2017/7/14/Costa-Rica-abre-el-camino- hacia-el-fin-de-los-pl-sticos-de-un-solo-uso.html.

Hahn E., et al. "Occupational Acroosteolysis in Vinyl Chloride Workers in Israel." *Israel Journal Medical Sciences* 15 (1979) 218–22.

Harvey, Fiona. "EU Rules out Tax on Plastic Products to Reduce Waste." *The Guardian* (October 2017). www.theguardian.com/environment/2017/oct/06/eu-rules-out-tax-on-plastic-products- to-reduce-waste.

Hoet, P., and D. Lison. "Ototoxicity of Toluene and Styrene: State of Current Knowledge." *Critical Review of Toxicology* 20 (2008) 127–70.

Holmes, L. A., et al. "Adsorption of Trace Metals to Plastic Resin Pellets in the Marine Environment." *Environmental Pollution* 160 (2012) 42–48.

Hood, Laura. "Biodiversity: Facts and Figures." (August 2010). https://www.scidev.net/global/biodiversity/feature/biodiversity-facts-and-figures-1.html

Hoover, Elizabeth, et al. "Indigenous Peoples of North America: Environmental Exposures and Reproductive Justice." *Environmental Health Perspectives* 120 (2012) 1645.

Hopewell, Jefferson, et al. "Plastics Recycling: Challenges and Opportunities." *Philosophical Transactions of the Royal Society B: Biological Sciences* 364 (2009) 2115–26.

"How Many U.S. Deaths Are Caused by Poverty, Lack of Education, and Other Social Factors?" Columbia University Mailman School of Public Health (July 2011). www.mailman.columbia.edu/public-health-now/news/how-many-us-deaths-are-caused-poverty-lack-education-and-other-social-factors.

"HP Announces Commitment to Create Sustainable Recycling Opportunities in Haiti." *HP News* (September 2016). www8.hp.com/us/en/hp-news/press-  release.html?id=2332945&jumpid=reg_r1002_usen_c-001_title_r0010.

Hunt, Patricia A., et al. "Bisphenol A Exposure Causes Meiotic Aneuploidy in the Female Mouse." *Current Biology* 13 (2003) 546–53.

Hussain, Nasir, et al. "Recent Advances in the Understanding of Uptake of Microparticulates Across the Gastrointestinal Lymphatics." *Advanced Drug Delivery Reviews* 50 (2001) 107–42.

Hyde, L. *The Gift: Imagination and the Erotic Life of Property*. New York: Random House 1983.

"Ikea to Use Packaging Made from Mushrooms That Will Decompose in a Garden Within Weeks." *National Post* (February 2016). https://nationalpost.com/news/world/ikea-fungus-mushrooms-for-packaging.

"The Impact of the Use of 'Oxo-Degradable' Plastic on the Environment." European Commission DG Environment (2016). www.cobro.org.pl/images/__doc__/polecamy/oxo-degradowalne-en.pdf+.

Intagliata, Christoper. "Whale Poop Drives Global Nutrient Cycling". *Scientific American* (October 2015). https://www.scientificamerican.com/podcast/episode/whale-poop-drives-global-nutrient-cycling/

Kasirajan, Subrahmaniyan, and Mathieu Ngouajio. "Polyethylene and Biodegradable Mulches for Agricultural Applications: A Review." *Agronomy for Sustainable Development* 32 (2012) 501–29.

Kent, R. T., et al. "Subsurface Injection in Ontario, Canada." In *Proceedings of the International Symposium on Subsurface Injection of Liquid Wastes*, 380–97. Dublin, OH: National Water Well Association, 1968.

Khan, Sehroon, et al. "Biodegradation of Polyester Polyurethane by *Aspergillus tubingensis*." *Environmental Pollution* 225 (2017) 469–80.

Kirstein, Inga V., et al. "Dangerous Hitchhikers? Evidence for Potentially Pathogenic Vibrio Spp. on Microplastic Particles." *Marine Environmental Research* 120 (2016) 1–8.

Klauder, D. S., and H. G. Petering. "Protective Value of Dietary Copper and Iron against

Some Toxic Effects of Lead in Rats." *Environmental Health Perspectives* 12 (1975) 77–80.

Klimentidis, Yann C. et al. "Canaries in the Coal Mine: A Cross-Species Analysis of the Plurality of Obesity Epidemics." *Proceedings of the Royal Society B: Biological Sciences* 278 (2011) 1626–1632.

Krishnan, Aruna V., et al. "Bisphenol-A: An Estrogenic Substance is Released from Polycarbonate Flasks During Autoclaving." *Endocrinology* 132 (1993) 2279–86.

Kumar, Sahni, et al. "Screening of Poly Vinyl Chloride Degrading Bacteria from Plastic Contaminated Area of Baddi." *Journal of Applied Pharmaceutical Research* 5 (2017) 34–7.

Lai, Juvina. "Taiwan to Ban All Cosmetics Containing Microbeads." *Taiwan News* (August 2017), www.taiwannews.com.tw/en/news/3225656.

Laville, Sandra. "Coca-Cola Increased Its Production of Plastic Bottles by a Billion Last

Year, Says Greenpeace." *The Guardian* (October 2017). www.theguardian. com/environment/2017/oct/02/coca-cola-increased-its-production- of-plastic-bottles-by-a-billion-last-year-say-greenpeace.

Laville, Sandra, and Matthew Taylor. "A Million Bottles a Minute: World's Plastic Binge 'as Dangerous as Climate Change'." *The Guardian* (June 2017). www. theguardian.com/environment/2017/jun/28/a-million-a-minute-worlds-plastic-bottle-binge-as-dangerous-as-climate-change.

Le, Hoa H., et al. "Bisphenol A Is Released from Polycarbonate Drinking Bottles and Mimics the Neurotoxic Actions of Estrogen in Developing Cerebellar Neurons." *Toxicology Letters* 176 (2008) 149–56.

Li, De-Kun, et al., "Urine Bisphenol-A (BPA) Level in Relation to Semen Quality." *Fertility and Sterility* 95 (2011) 625–30.

Liebezeit, Gerd, and Elisabeth Liebezeit. "Non-Pollen Particulates in Honey and Sugar." *Food Additives & Contaminants: Part A* 30 (2013) 2136–40.

———. "Synthetic Particles as Contaminants in German Beers." *Food Additives & Contaminants: Part A* 31 (2014) 1574–78.

Ling, S. D., et al. "Ubiquity of Microplastics in Coastal Seafloor Sediments." *Marine Pollution Bulletin* 121 (2017) 104–10.

"List by Country; Bag Charges, Taxes, and Bans." http://www.bigfatbags.co.uk/bans-taxes-charges-plastic-bags/.

Loerch, S. C. "Efficacy of Plastic Pot Scrubbers as a Replacement for Roughage in High- Concentrate Cattle Diets." *Journal of Animal Science* 69 (1991) 321–28.

MacDonald, Elaine., and Sarah. Rang. "Exposing Canada's Chemical Valley: An Investigation of Cumulative Air Pollution Emissions in the Sarnia, Ontario Area." An Ecojustice Report (2007). http://www.ecojustice. ca/publications/reports/report-exposing-canadas-chemical-valley/attachment.

MacEachern, Diane. "Styrofoam Bans are Sweeping Across the Nation." https://storyofstuff.org/blog/styrofoam-bans-are-sweeping-across-the-nation/.

Mackenzie, C.A. et al. "Declining Sex Ratio in a First Nation Community." *Environmental Health Perspectives* 113 (2005) 1295–98.

Mallow, E. B., and M. A. Fox. "Phthalates and Critically Ill Neonates: Device-Related Exposures and Non-Endocrine Toxic Risks." *Journal of Perinatology* 34 (2014) 892–97.

Mankiewicz, Paul S. *Artificial soil*. United States Patent 6946496 B2 filed Sep 23, 2003 and issued Sep 20, 2005.

"Man-Made Fibres and Plastic Found in the Deepest Living Organisms." *Newcastle University Press Office* (November 2017). www.ncl.ac.uk/press/articles/archive/2017/11/plasticocean/.

"Map of Campaigns." https://www.banthebottle.net/map-of-campaigns/.

Mariscal-Arcas, M., et al. "Dietary Exposure Assessment of Pregnant Women to Bisphenol- A from Cans and Microwave Containers in Southern Spain." *Food Chemistry Toxicology* 47 (2009) 506–10.

Matkin, O. A. "Perlite vs. Polystyrene in Potting Mixes." *The Schundler Company*. www.schundler.com/polystyrene.htm.

Mato, Yukie, et al. "Plastic Resin Pellets as a Transport Medium for Toxic Chemicals in the Marine Environment." *Environmental Science & Technology* 31 (2001) 318–24.

Mattsson, K., et al. "Brain Damage and Behavioural Disorders in Fish Induced by Plastic Nanoparticles Delivered through the Food Chain." *Scientific Reports* 7 (2017) 11452.

McAloose, Denise, and Alisa L. Newton. "Wildlife Cancer: a Conservation Perspective." *Nature Reviews Cancer* 9 (2009) 518–26.

McDonald, G. Reid, et al. "Bioactive Contaminants Leach from Disposable Laboratory Plasticware." *Science* 322 (2008) 917.

Mercea, P. "Physicochemical Processes Involved in Migration of Bisphenol A from Polycarbonate." *Journal of Applied Polymer Science* 112 (2009) 579–93.

"Mid-Ocean Plastics Cleanup Schemes: Too Little Too Late?" http://www.algalita.org/mid-ocean-plastics-cleanup-schemes-too-little-too-late/.

Millar W.J., and B.H. Gerry. "Childhood Asthma." *Health Reports* 10 (1998) 12.

Minter, Adam. "The Burning Truth Behind an E-waste Dump in Africa." *Smithsonian* (January 2016). https://www.smithsonianmag.com/science-nature/burning-truth-behind-e-waste-dump-africa-180957597/.

———. "Plastic, Poverty and Pollution in China's Recycling Dead Zone." *The Guardian* (July 2014). https://www.theguardian.com/lifeandstyle/2014/jul/16/plastic-poverty-pollution-china-recycling-dead-zone.

Mittelstaedt, Martin. "Researchers Raise Alarm after Chemical Leak Found in Common Plastic." *Globe and Mail* (November 2008). https://www.theglobeandmail.com/news/national/researchers-raise-alarm-after-chemical-leak-found-in-common-plastic/article1065340/.

Mitro, Susanna D., et al. "Consumer Product Chemicals in Indoor Dust: A Quantitative Meta-analysis of U.S. Studies." *Environmental Science & Technology* 50 (2016) 10661–72.

Mock, Brentin. "How Environmental Injustice Connects to Police Violence." (July 2016). http://www.citylab.com/politics/2016/07/how-environmental-injustice-connects-to-police-violence/492053/.

Mooney, Chris. "Ocean Trash Isn't Just Bad for the Environment—It's Bad for Your State of Mind." *The Washington Post* (July 2015). https://www.washingtonpost.com/news/energy-environment/wp/2015/07/08/why-clean-beaches-are-so-important-if-you-want-a-relaxing-vacation/?noredirect=on&utm_term=.3cb33f2cc69d.

Moore, Thomas. "Sky to Remove All Single-Use Plastics by 2020." *Sky News* (October 2017). news.sky.com/story/sky-to-remove-all-single-use-plastics-by-2020–11067415.

Morrison, Dan, and Chris Tyree. "Invisibles: The Plastic Inside Us." *Orb.* www.orbmedia.org/stories/Invisibles_plastics.

Moskin, Julia. "Superfood or Monster from the Deep?" *New York Times* (September 2008). www.nytimes.com/2008/09/17/dining/17nutrients.html?mcubz=0.

Moudgal, Sandeep. "Total Plastic Ban in Karnataka." *The Times of India* (March 2016). timesofindia.indiatimes.com/city/bengaluru/Total-plastic-ban-in-Karnataka/articleshow/51397198.cms.

Mühlschlegel, Peter, et al. "Lack of Evidence for Microplastic Contamination in Honey."

*Food Additives & Contaminants. Part A, Chemistry, Analysis, Control, Exposure & Risk Assessment* 34 (2017) 1982–89.

Myers, C. *The Biblical Vision of Sabbath Economics* (Tell the Word). Washington, D.C.: Church of the Saviour, 2001.

Nakashima, Etsuko, et al. "Quantification of Toxic Metals Derived from Macroplastic Litter on Ookushi Beach, Japan." *Environmental Science & Technology* 46 (2012 10099–105.

"National Children's Study (NCS)." https://www.nichd.nih.gov/research/NCS/Pages/default.aspx.

"National Health and Nutrition Examination Survey." https://www.cdc.gov/nchs/nhanes/index.htm

Nerin, C., et al. "Compounds From Multilayer Plastic Bags Cause Reproductive Failures in Artificial Insemination." *Scientific Reports* 4 (2014) 4913.

Newbold, R.R., et al. "Developmental exposure to endocrine disruptors and the obesity epidemic." *Reproductive Toxicology* 23, (2007) 290–296.

———."Developmental exposure to estrogenic compounds and obesity." *Birth Defects Research Part A. Clinical and Molecular Teratology* 73 (2005) 478–80.

———."Perinatal exposure to environmental estrogens and the development of obesity." *Molecular Nutrition & Food Research* 51 (2007) 912–17.

"The New Plastics Economy: Rethinking the Future of Plastics." *Ellen MacArthur*

*Foundation* (January 2016). www.ellenmacarthurfoundation.org/publications/
the-new-
plastics-economy-rethinking-the-future-of-plastics.

*The New Plastics Economy*. Ellen MacArthur Foundation (March 2016).
www.ellenmacarthurfoundation.org/assets/downloads/
EllenMacArthurFoundation_
TheNewPlasticsEconomy_15-3-16.pdf.

"No More Deaths." (September 2017). forms.nomoredeaths.org/wp-content/
uploads/2017/09/ Newsletter-2017fall-v2-esp-color.pdf.

Nowlan, Linda. "An international plastics treaty could avert a "Silent Spring"
for our seas." *The Conversation* (February 2018). https://theconversation.
com/an-international-plastics-treaty-could-avert-a-silent-spring-for-
our-seas-90990.

Oberbeckmann, Sonja, et al. "Marine Microplastic-Associated Biofilms—a
Review." *Environmental Chemistry* 12 (2015) 551–62.

Oberlies, N.H., et al. "Microbial-mediated Release of Bisphenol A from
Polycarbonate Vessels. *Letters in Applied Microbiology* 46 (2008) 271–75.

"The Ocean Cleanup." https://www.theoceancleanup.com/about/.

Ocean Conservancy. *Stemming the Tide: Land-Based Strategies for a Plastic-
Free Ocean.* (2015). oceanconservancy.org/wp-content/uploads/2017/04/
full-report-stemming-the.pdf.

O'Connell, S. G., et al. "Silicone Wristbands as Personal Passive Samplers."
*Environmental Science and Technology* 48 (2014) 3327–35.

Olivieri, Aldo, et al. "On the Disruption of Biochemical and Biological Assays by
Chemicals Leaching from Disposable Laboratory Plasticware."*Canadian
Journal of Physiology and Pharmacology* 90 (2012) 697–703.

"Operation Clean Sweep." https://www.nurdlehunt.org.uk/whats-the-solution.
html.

Orci, Taylor. "Are Tea Bags Turning Us Into Plastic?" *The Atlantic* (April 2013).
www.theatlantic.com/health/archive/2013/04/are-tea-bags-turning-us-into-
plastic/274482/.

"Oregon Refuse and Recycling Association Fact Sheet." (September 2017).
www.orra.net/wp-content/uploads/2017/09/China-Recyclables-Ban-
Fact-Sheet_ORRA_September-2017.pdf.

Oxo-Biodegradable Plastics Association, "Preventing Oceans of Plastic Soup."
(March 2016). www.biodeg.org/page31.html.

———."Standards for Testing Oxo-Biodegradable Plastics." http://www.
biodeg.org/standards.html.

Paben, Jared. "China Announces 'Sword' Crackdown on Illegal Scrap Plastic
Imports." *Plastics Recycling Update* (June 2017). https://resource-recycling.
com/plastics/2017/02/15/china-announces-sword-crackdown-	illegal-
scrap-plastic-imports/.

Paben, Jared. "End User of Recovered PE Film Reports Earnings Boost."
*Plastics Recycling Update* (November 2017). https://resource- recycling.

com/plastics/2017/11/08/end-user-recovered-pe-film-reports-earnings-boost/.

Paine, Robert T. "Food Web Complexity and Species Diversity." *The American Naturalist* 100 (1966) 65–75.

Pascal, Viel, et al. "New Concept to Remove Heavy Metals from Liquid Waste Based on Electrochemical PH-Switchable Immobilized Ligands." *Applied Surface Science* 253 (2007) 3263–69.

Pennington, James. "Every Minute, One Garbage Truck of Plastic Is Dumped into Our Oceans. This Has to Stop." *World Economic Forum* (October 2016). www.weforum.org/agenda/2016/10/every-minute-one-garbage-truck-of-plastic-is- dumped-into-our-oceans/.

Peplow, Mark. "Hormone Disruptors Rise from the Dead." *Nature News* (September 2013). www.nature.com/news/hormone-disruptors-rise-from-the-dead-1.13831.

"Phase-out of lightweight plastic bags." https://en.wikipedia.org/wiki/Phase-out_of_lightweight_plastic_bags.

"Piñatex." https://www.ananas-anam.com.

"Plant Bottle." https://www.coca-colacompany.com/plantbottle-technology.

"Plastic Disclosure Project." http://plasticdisclosure.org/.

"Plastic Pollution Coalition." http://www.plasticpollutioncoalition.org/take-action-1/.

"Pledges Galore." https://www.lifewithoutplastic.com/store/ca/pledges_galore#.W3401i2ZORs.

"Polythene Choking Drains, Water Bodies for Lack of Monitoring." *The Daily Star* (August 2011). www.thedailystar.net/news-detail-198253.

Pope Francis. "Laudato si." (May 2015). http://w2.vatican.va/content/francesco/en/encyclicals/documents/papa-francesco_20150524_enciclica-laudato-si.html.

Preston, B. J., et al. "Clinical Aspects of Vinyl Chloride Disease: Acro-Osteolysis." *Proceedings of the Royal Society of Medicine* 69 (1976) 284–86.

Provencher, J. F., et al. "Garbage in Guano? Microplastic Debris Found in Faecal Precursors of Seabirds Known to Ingest Plastics." *Science of the Total Environment* 644 (2018) 1477–84.

Pullman, Nina. "Swedish Supermarkets Replace Sticky Labels with Laser Marking." *The Guardian* (January 2017). www.theguardian.com/sustainable-business/2017/jan/16/ms-and-swedish-supermarkets-ditch-sticky-labels-for-natural-branding.

"PVC and DEHP in Neonatal Intensive Care Units." Kaiser Permanente/Health Care Without Harm. https://noharm-uscanada.org/sites/default/files/documents-files/97/Case_Study_PVC_NICU_ Kaiser.pdf

Quilliam, Richard S., et al. "Seaweeds and Plastic Debris Can Influence the Survival of Faecal Indicator Organisms in Beach Environments." *Marine Pollution Bulletin* 84 (2014) 201–07.

Reed, Casey E., and Suzanne E. Fenton. "Exposure to Diethylstilbestrol during Sensitive Life Stages: A Legacy of Heritable Health Effects." *Birth Defects Research Part C, Embryo Today: Reviews* 99 (2013) 134–46.

Riskey, Erin. "Which Countries Have Banned Plastic Bags?" (November 2017). https://study.com/blog/which-countries-have-banned-plastic-bags.html.

Rochester, Johanna R., and Ashley L. Bolden. "Bisphenol S and F: A Systematic Review and Comparison of the Hormonal Activity of Bisphenol A Substitutes." *Environmental Health Perspectives* 123 (2015) 643.

Rochman, Chelsea, et al. "Anthropogenic Debris in Seafood: Plastic Debris and Fibers from Textiles in Fish and Bivalves Sold for Human Consumption." *Nature Scientific Reports* 5 (2015) 14340.

———."The Ecological Impacts of Marine Debris: Unraveling the Demonstrated Evidence from What Is Perceived." *Ecology* 97 (2016) 302–12.

———."Ingested Plastic Transfers Hazardous Chemicals to Fish and Induces Hepatic Stress." *Nature Scientific Reports* 3 (2013) 3263.

Romeo, T., et al. "First Evidence of Presence of Plastic Debris in Stomach of Large Pelagic Fish in the Mediterranean Sea." *Marine Pollution Bulletin,* 95 (2015) 358–61.

Rudel, Ruthann A., et al. "Food Packaging and Bisphenol A and Bis(2-Ethyhexyl) Phthalate Exposure: Findings from a Dietary Intervention." *Environmental Health Perspectives* 119 (2011) 914–20.

Russell, Jonathan R, et al. "Biodegradation of Polyester Polyurethane by Endophytic Fungi." *Applied Environmental Microbiology* 77 (2011) 6076–84.

Sapkota, Amy R., et al. "What Do We Feed to Food-Production Animals? A Review of Animal Feed Ingredients and Their Potential Impacts on Human Health." *Environmental Health Perspectives* 115 (2007) 663–70.

Schell, Orville. *Modern Meat: Antibiotics, Hormones, and the Pharmaceutical Farm.* New York: Random House, 1984.

Schulz, Laura C. "The Dutch Hunger Winter and the Developmental Origins of Health and Disease. *Proceedings of the National Academy of Sciences* 107 (2010) 16757–58.

Schuster, P. F., et al. "Permafrost Stores a Globally Significant Amount of Mercury." *Geophysical Research Letters* 45, (2018) 1463–71.

"Seabin Project." http://seabinproject.com.

"Sea turtle with straw up its nostril—"no" to plastic straws." (August 2015). https://www.youtube.com/watch?v=4wH878t78bw.

Self, Deb. "Marinas, Boaters Need to Take Leadership on Bay Pollution." *San Francisco Baykeeper* (March 2012). baykeeper.org/news/column/marinas-boaters-need-take-leadership-bay-pollution.

Senyek, M.L., et al. *Dibenzyltrithiocarbonate Molecular Weight Regulator for Emulsion Polymerization.* US Patent 6369158 filed Dec. 22, 1999. https://www.google.com/patents/US6369158

Shah, Aamer Ali et al. "Biological Degradation of Plastics: A Comprehensive Review." *Biotechnology Advances* 26 (2008) 246–65.

Shah, Anup. "Poverty Stats and Facts." http://www.globalissues.org/article/26/poverty-facts-and-stats.

Sharma, Arpita, et al. "Circadian Rhythm Disruption: Health Consequences." *Biological Rhythm Research* 47 (2016) 191–213.

Shuping, Niu, and Ken Wills. "Plastic Film Covering 12% of China's Farmland Pollutes Soil." *Bloomberg News* (September 2017). www.bloomberg.com/news/articles/2017–09-05/plastic-film-covering-12-of-china-s-farmland-contaminates-soil.

Simoneau, C., et al. "Comparison of Migration from Polyethersulphone and Polycarbonate Baby Bottles." *Food Additives & Contaminants: Part A* 28 (2011) 1763–68.

Skipping Rocks Lab. "Ooho!" http://www.skippingrockslab.com/ooho!.html.

Smith, Betty. *A Tree Grows in Brooklyn.* New York: Harper & Brothers, 1943.

Snowden, E. and Fanshawe, F. "Beachwatch 2007—The 15th Annual Beach Litter Survey Report." *Marine Conservation Society Ross-on-Wye, UK* (2008). www.adoptabeach.org.uk.

"Some 385 Million Children Live in Extreme Poverty, World Bank-UNICEF Study Reveals." *UN News Centre* (October 2016). www.un.org/apps/news/story.asp?NewsID=55198.

Soto, Ana, et al. "P-Nonyl-phenol: An Estrogenic Xenobiotic Released from 'Modified'

Polystyrene." *Environmental Health Perspectives* 92 (1991) 167–73.

"State Plastic and Paper Bag Legislation." (May 2018). http://www.ncsl.org/research/environment-and-natural-resources/plastic-bag-legislation.aspx.

Staub, Colin. "Diverse Group Aligns in Opposition to Oxo-Degradables." *Plastics Recycling Update* (November 2017). https://resource- recycling.com/plastics/2017/11/08/diverse-group-aligns-opposition-oxo-degradables/.

Stephen, Michael. "In My Opinion: Consider the Benefits of Oxo-Biodegradables." *Plastics Recycling Update* (November 2017). https://resource- recycling.com/plastics/2017/11/08/opinion-consider-benefits-oxo-biodegradables/.

"Styrene." *Report on Carcinogens, Fourteenth Edition.* ntp.niehs.nih.gov/ntp/roc/content /profiles/styrene.pdf.

*Supersize Me!* Directed by Morgan Spurlock. Samuel Goldwyn Films Roadside Attractions (2004).

Suzuki, T., et al. "Prenatal and Neonatal Exposure to Bisphenol-A Enhances the Central Dopamine D1 Receptor-Mediated Action in Mice: Enhancement of the Methamphetamine-Induced Abuse State." *Neuroscience* 117 (2003) 639.

Suzuki, Takeji, and Hiroshi Azuma. *Artificial Soil and Process for Producing the Same.* US Patent 5312661 A filed Sep 13, 1991 and issued May 17, 1994.

Taylor, Matthew. "Coffee Shops Not Doing Enough to Combat Huge Increase in Waste Cups." *The Guardian* (October 2017). www.theguardian.com/environment/2017/oct/10/coffee-shops-not-doing-enough-to- combat-huge-increase-in-wasted-cups.

———."Sewage Plants Are Leaking Millions of Tiny Plastic Beads into Britain's Seas." *The Guardian* (October 2017). www.theguardian.com/environment/2017/oct/11/sewage-plants-are-leaking-millions- of-tiny-plastic-beads-into-britains-seas.

Teimouri Sendesi, Seyedeh Mahboobeh, et al. "Worksite Chemical Air Emissions and Worker Exposure during Sanitary Sewer and Stormwater Pipe Rehabilitation Using Cured-in-Place-Pipe (CIPP)." *Environmental Science & Technology Letters* 4 (2017) 325–33.

Teuten, Emma L., et al. "Potential for Plastics to Transport Hydrophobic Contaminants."

*Environmental Science and Technology* 41 (2007) 7759–64.

Tkavc, Rok, et al. "Prospects for Fungal Bioremediation of Acidic Radioactive Waste Sites: Characterization and Genome Sequence of *Rhodotorula taiwanensis* MD1149." *Frontiers in Microbiology* 8 (2018) 2528.

Tosetto, Louise, et al. "Microplastics on Beaches: Ingestion and Behavioural Consequences for Beachhoppers."*Marine Biology* 163 (2016) 199.

"ToxFAQs for Di(2-ethylhexyl)phthalate (DEHP)." *Agency for Toxic Substances and Disease Registry* (September 2002). www.atsdr.cdc.gov/toxfaqs/tf.asp?id=377&tid=65.

Traore, Assitan Sylla. "Gender and Plastic Bag Pollution: Consumption, Globalization, and Environmental Justice in Mali." Master's Thesis, University of Oregon, 2014.

Tullo, Alexander H. "The Cost of Plastic Packaging." *Chemical and Engineering News* 94 (2016) 32–37.

"'Turn the tide on plastic' urges UN, as microplastics in the seas now outnumber stars in our galaxy." *UN News Centre* (February 2017). http://www.un.org/apps/news/ story.asp?NewsID=56229#.WjweFiOZORs.

Tyree, Chris, and Dan Morrison. "Invisibles." *Orb.* orbmedia.org/stories/Invisibles_plastics /multimedia.

Ulloa, Astrid. "Perspectives of Environmental Justice from Indigenous Peoples of Latin America: A Relational Indigenous Environmental Justice." *Environmental Justice* 10 (2017) 175–80.

"United Nations Declares War on Ocean Plastic." *UNEP News Centre* (February 2017). web.unep.org/newscentre/un-declares-war-ocean-plastic.

United Nations Environment Programme. "Marine Litter, an analytical overview." *UNEP Document Repository Home* (2005). http://wedocs.unep.org/handle/20.500.11822/8348.

"An Update on Microfiber Pollution." https://www.patagonia.com/blog/2017/02/an-update-on-microfiber-pollution/.

"USGS Current Water Data for the Nation." https://waterdata.usgs.gov/nwis/rt.

Van Cauwenberghe, L., and Janssen, C. R. "Microplastics in Bivalves Cultured for Human Consumption." *Environmental Pollution* 193 (2014) 65–70.

Vianna, N.J., et al. "Angiosarcoma of the Liver: A Signal Lesion of Vinyl Chloride Exposure." *Environmental Health Perspectives* 41 (1981) 207–10.

Viñas P, et al. "Comparison of Two Derivatization-based Methods for Solid-phase Microextraction-Gas Chromatography–Mass Spectrometric Determination of Bisphenol A, Bisphenol S and Bisphenol Migrated from Food Cans." *Analytical and Bioanalytical Chemistry* 397 (2010) 115–25.

"Vinyl chloride." https://www.epa.gov/sites/production/files/2016-09/documents/vinyl-chloride.pdf.

Vivacqua, Adele, et al. "The Food Contaminants Bisphenol A and 4-Nonylphenol Act as
Agonists for Estrogen Receptor α in MCF7 Breast Cancer Cells." *Endocrine* 22 (2003) 275–84.

Volkheimer, Gerhard. "Hematogenous Dissemination of Ingested Polyvinyl Chloride
Particles." *Annals of the New York Academy of Sciences* 246 (1975) 164–71.

Von Goetz, N, et al. "Bisphenol A: How the Most Relevant Exposure Sources Contribute to Total Consumer Exposure." *Risk Analysis* 30 (2010) 473–87.

Wagner, Martin, and Jörg Oehlmann. "Endocrine Disruptors in Bottled Mineral Water: Total Estrogenic Burden and Migration from Plastic Bottles." *Environmental Science and Pollution Research International* 16 (2009) 278–86.

Wassener, Bettina. "Raising Awareness of Plastic Waste." *The New York Times* (August 2011). http://www.nytimes.com/2011/08/15/business/energy-environment/raising-awareness-of-plastic-waste.html.

Weisman, Alan. "Polymers Are Forever." *Orion Magazine* (2007). orionmagazine.org/article/polymers-are-forever/.

Welch, J. G. "Physical Parameters of Fiber Affecting Passage from the Rumen." *Journal of Dairy Science* 69 (1986) 2750–54.

Whetsell, M. S., et al. "Influence of Mass of Ruminal Contents on Voluntary Intake and Digesta Passage in Steers Fed a Forage and a Concentrate Diet." *Journal of Animal Science* 82 (2004) 1806–17.

White, T. W., and W. L. Reynolds. "Various Sources and Levels of Roughage in Steer Rations." *Journal of Animal Science* 28 (1969) 705–10.

Wick, Peter, et al. "Barrier Capacity of Human Placenta for Nanosized Materials." *Environmental Health Perspectives* 118 (2010) 432.

Wright, Stephanie L., et al. "Microplastic Ingestion Decreases Energy Reserves in Marine Worms." *Current Biology* 23 (2013) R1031–33.

Yang, Dongqi, et al. "Microplastic Pollution in Table Salts from China." *Environmental
Science & Technology* 49 (2015) 13622–27.

Yoshida, Shosuke, et al. "A Bacterium That Degrades and Assimilates Poly(Ethylene Terephthalate)." *Science* 351 (2016) 1196–99.

Zalko, Daniel, et al. "Viable Skin Efficiency Absorbs and Metabolizes Bisphenol A."
*Chemosphere* 82 (2011) 424–30.
Zettler, Erik R., et al. "Life in the 'Plastisphere': Microbial Communities on Plastic Marine Debris." *Environmental Science & Technology* 47 (2013) 7137–46.